P

MW00473595

MIDLIFE EMERGENCE: FREE YOUR INNER FIRE

Beyond an intricate portrait of self-discovery, this is a beautiful tribute to living a whole-hearted life. Berlingo—who acknowledges giving away her power for years to conventional expectations of love, marriage, and self-actualization—speaks with a deep wisdom that will resonate with any reader struggling to understand their unmet needs. She honors the fluidity of gender, sexuality, and human relationships in general, while using her personal experiences as a blueprint to "to write my own rule book for my life as an adult." Her words are almost poetic in their urgency to help readers navigate their own transitions.

BOOKLIFE BY PUBLISHERS WEEKLY

A riveting, poetic, and thunderously courageous book! It's a deep dive into radical honesty. Every woman is offered a sacred invitation in midlife, and Jen's ability to articulate her journey and share the amazing opportunity that this precious time offers acts as a reframe on a view that need not be limiting, but full of magic and transformation. I am ever so grateful for this offering!

CARRÉ OTIS   MODEL, MOTHER, ACTIVIST, AND AUTHOR OF *BEAUTY, DISRUPTED: A MEMOIR*

Poetically written with vulnerability, wisdom, and humor, Jen Berlingo beautifully reframes the masculine archetype of the *midlife crisis* into an inspiring tale of the feminine *midlife emergence*. Jen does a seamless job of weaving together personal story and useful theory, while guiding you through your own exploration of the rite of passage women undergo in the second half of life. This book is a must-read for any woman looking to shed their conditioning and reclaim their authentic expression of self and sexuality.

JESSICA FERN PSYCHOTHERAPIST AND BESTSELLING AUTHOR OF *POLYSECURE: ATTACHMENT, TRAUMA AND CONSENSUAL NONMONOGAMY*

This book is for every woman who wants more in her life and doesn't quite know how to get it. Jen's story is the ultimate reminder that living in our authentic truth, no matter how difficult the road may seem, is the recipe for a beautiful life. Jen shares her wisdom so vulnerably and offers the reader a road map to true and lasting transformation.

KEELE BURGIN INTERNATIONAL BESTSELLING AUTHOR OF *WHOLLY UNRAVELED: A MEMOIR*

Written with depth, color, and candor, *Midlife Emergence* is one woman's utterly human portrayal of becoming who she *really* is. Jen's courageous revelations, humor, and accessibility invite us to similarly align with truth, while also providing clever and creative exercises to help us do so—a true gem and an inspiring read.

ERIC MEYERS ASTROLOGER AND AUTHOR OF *THE ASTROLOGY OF AWAKENING*

For anyone who has found themselves reexamining their sexuality later in life, this book provides deeply satisfying answers to the questions of "Why me?" and "Why now?" *Midlife Emergence* is a thoughtful weaving of Jen's own captivating story with the social science behind why we do some of the things we do. It's a lesson in appreciating the challenging process of transformation.

JILLIAN ABBY AUTHOR OF *PERFECTLY QUEER*

"*More* is perhaps the most subversive thing a middle-aged woman can claim." This line from *Midlife Emergence* jumped off the page and landed in my body solidly, the way only profound truth really can. To live into the fullness of the second half of our lives, we have to be willing to want, name, and claim MORE. We must not only have the courage to acknowledge that steady drumbeat of knowing that whispers "there is more," but the audacity to follow it where it leads. In this book, Jen skillfully weaves personal memoir with her background in psychotherapy to create a powerful guide through the liminal spaces of midlife.

JEANETTE LEBLANC AUTHOR OF *YOU ARE NOT TOO MUCH*

If you are a midlife woman who is feeling a deep call for change, Jen's teaching memoir is a nourishing and empowering book to curl up to. She shares her own powerful story of emergence and in doing so invites us to find and claim our own.

BARI TESSLER SOMATIC PSYCHOTHERAPIST AND AUTHOR OF *THE ART OF MONEY*

Watching Jen Berlingo take off in her life is sort of like watching one of those fireworks that starts out very sweetly in the twinkle zone, but then, hey look! It executes a surprising explosion, and you follow that up into the night sky and then it shoots beauty to every part of your vision, and you shout with sheer astonishment at the freedom of it. A guidebook for women who suspect they want more and are ready to start claiming it.

LISA JONES   AUTHOR OF THE AWARD-WINNING
MEMOIR *BROKEN: A LOVE STORY*

midlife
emergence

midlife emergence

free your inner fire

jen berlingo

**BOLD
STORY
PRESS**
WASHINGTON, DC

First edition: April 2023
Library of Congress Control Number: 2022922501

ISBN: 978-1-954805-46-0 (paperback)
ISBN: 978-1-954805-47-7 (e-book)

Text and cover design by KP Design
Original cover painting by Jen Berlingo
Author photo by Jewel Afflerbaugh

"So What?" Composed by Ani DiFranco. Righteous Babe Music (BMI). All rights reserved. Reprinted by permission.

Extract from the poem "Käthe Kollwitz" from *The Collected Poems of Muriel Rukeyser* by Muriel Rukeyser. Copyright © 2006 by Muriel Rukeyser. Reprinted by permission of ICM Partners.

"Wild Geese" by Mary Oliver. Reprinted by the permission of The Charlotte Sheedy Literary Agency as agent for the author. Copyright © 1986, 2003, 2006, 2017 by Mary Oliver with permission of Bill Reichblum.

Excerpt from "Rewilding Female Culture" by Christiane Pelmas. From https://www.christianepelmas.com/vc-3-hour
-immersions/rewilding-female-culture. June 2019.

Printed in the United States of America
10 9 8 7 6 5 4 3 2 1

For generations forward and backward
in my own lineage, and in yours.

*The story you're ashamed to tell is
the one that will set you free.*

LIZZY RUSSINKO

contents

author's note

The events in this book are my truth and are told to the best of my recollection. Some identifying circumstances have been changed to protect the privacy of the individuals involved. While the dialogue may not be verbatim, the spirit and essence reflect how these conversations occurred and how I understood them. I recognize that my worldview is not universal and that my personal take on what has happened in my life is simply one lens. I can only speak from my lived experience.

introduction

Life really begins at forty.
Up until then, you are just doing research.

CARL JUNG

MAGMA
March 2017

The year I was forty-one years old, I sensed a shift in my being. It was as though a tectonic process had taken over my solid, internal landscape, moving the plates of my identity enough to expose peeks at my molten core. Much like a dormant volcano, from the outside my life appeared stable, peaceful, and lush, but a fiery magma brewed deep within, yearning to see the light of day. I had kept this inner fire bound, as I was terrified of its capacity to obliterate my entire village.

At the time, I lived what many would consider to be a pretty sweet life. I was several years into working in my private psychotherapy practice in the San Francisco Bay Area. I lived in a sprawling, California ranch home with one of those large, trendy swan rafts floating in our back-yard pool. Our inflatable swan was named Juno, after the Greek goddess of marriage. I was nestled into this life alongside my loving, generous, devoted husband, Craig, to whom I'd been married for fourteen years, our vibrant ten-year-old daughter, and two chatty, snuggly cats. Craig was an executive in Silicon Valley, and he was the primary breadwinner in our household. This allowed me to see my psychotherapy clients only during the hours our daughter was at school, so I could be with her when she was home. On weekends, the three of us would wade in starfish-laden tide pools along the Pacific coast, or we'd take our daughter to see a musical in the city and enjoy delicious Burmese food (with that amazing milk tea!). There was laughter, affection, nourishment, comfort, and love. On the surface, everything was humming along very smoothly, so much so that my mother-in-law often reflected that we made marriage look easy, and some of our friends regarded us as the healthiest married couple they knew.

I'd swat away dissatisfaction whenever it crept into my psyche, berating myself for not feeling grateful enough for this exquisite life. But still, an inner fire scorched my insides. Perhaps if I'd just gotten a stereotypical red sports car at the onset of my forties, the story you're about to read would be an entirely different tale. But, instead of a little red Corvette, in the winter of that year, I bought a sensible, small SUV that Craig affectionately dubbed my "midlife-crisis Honda." It was a fine car, but it didn't quell the quaking. *At all.*

I'm a total self-inquiry junkie, so I ached to excavate every vibrating layer of myself and dive headfirst into whatever this liquid fire underneath could teach me. I wasn't sure how to make contact with this amorphous discomfort. About a month into driving my midlife crisis Honda on errands around my palm-tree–lined neighborhood, I received a wax-sealed invitation in the mail. It was from a psychotherapy colleague in Boulder, Colorado, where I had completed Naropa University's master's program in transpersonal counseling psychology and art therapy in my late twenties. This handwritten note invited me into a four-month-long women's circle where we would unearth and reclaim our soul's purpose, finally embodying the gifts we were meant to offer to the world. Enclosed in the letter was a single owl feather, which I placed on my altar with a giggle, as I felt a bit like Harry Potter being summoned to Hogwarts with the promise of a more magical life. At first, I dismissed the invitation. It would mean I'd have to spend four very long weekends in Colorado away from my husband and daughter. Being away from my daughter for more than a night felt a little scary—and a lot self-indulgent.

Less than a week later, after a long stretch of back-to-back therapy clients, I sank into my office chair, absolutely spent. I knew I needed to bring more of myself to whatever the next iteration of my career would be, as one-sided therapeutic relationships had left me feeling invisible and burned out. This uneasiness inspired me to try to dig the invitation out of the giant recycling bin outside, where I thought I'd thrown it. When I didn't find it there, I surprised myself by breaking into a full-on, desperate sob. Halfway into this tearful trance, I walked over to my office bookshelf and somehow plucked the invitation out from between two random books, where I did not remember placing it. My jaw dropped, and I set the lovely parchment paper beside the owl feather on my altar.

That was just the sign I needed to commit to this intensive women's circle alongside a group of twenty other healing practitioners. The fact that this cohort would also include Emily, my best friend of fifteen years, was a major perk, as we could support each other through the experience. I was beyond thirsty for any guidance that would bring me to the depths of this unmet longing. I prayed it would satisfy the fiery eros coursing through my blood, bringing vitality and passion back into my career.[1] At the time, I had no idea that I would need to spend the next few years addressing my personal life as a prerequisite to realigning my vocational life.

GOLDEN
June 2017

During the first weekend intensive, the group of women formed our cushions and blankets into a circle inside a sacred temple in the stunning foothills of Boulder. The facilitator guided us into a visualization to invoke the image of an inner healer, which was meant to help us step into our power with greater intention. I saw my inner healer

---

1   Eros was one of the primordial gods who helped to bring creation into existence. In Greek mythology, Eros mated with Chaos, and life sprang forth into the light. The term *eros* goes beyond sexual love or lust to describe the potential life-force energy needed to create.

as a powerful empress, with wild hair of shining gold, streaked with silver strands of wisdom, and encircled by a gem-encrusted crown. She was mostly naked but casually draped herself in a low-cut, jewel-toned velvet, always revealing her red and magenta heart, glowing with a deep, expansive love. Her eyes were the gray-blue depth of the ocean, with rainbow magic twinkling within them, like the flash of a labradorite stone. She reflected healing energy via golden spangly discs glittering on and around her, like a million suns and moons. She gave off a vibe of being deeply rooted in the earth, while also being connected to the heavenly realms. Her magnetism captivated me— she embodied both the familiar comfort of home and the allure of an exotic, mysterious adventure.

When I heard the facilitator beating a drum to signify the ending of our journeys, I imagined this inner healer touching my face in a few places with the soft tip of her long, graceful finger. Anointing each touchpoint with gold, she seemed to initiate me into the next chapter of my life. The final place she touched was the left side of my nose. When I woke from my altered state, my nostril felt sore and hot, as though it had just been pierced. For days after, whenever I touched my face, I expected to feel a nose ring. After a month of feeling like this golden talisman was missing, I eventually took myself to a piercing studio, marking the rite of passage into the second act of my life.

A few years later, I discovered that nose piercings carry various meanings in cultures around the world. In the Middle East and in some African tribes, a husband gifts his wife with a golden nose ring as a form of insurance, with the idea that if he dies, she can sell the nose ring to provide for herself. According to the Indian science of Ayurveda, the left nostril is linked to female reproductive organs, so the piercing is said to make menstrual and labor pain more bearable. When nose piercings came to the West, punk rockers and goths adopted them as a defiant symbol of rebellion against conservative values while asserting personal independence. Yep, in hindsight, all that sounds like what I was up to. What I didn't know at the time of this penetrating induction was that I was preparing for stability after a divorce, the labor pains of birthing a publicly queer identity, and claiming my unconventional sovereignty in a culture that clings fearfully to convention. I was preparing for the vulnerability of being visible in my awkward navigation of midlife. That fiery golden ring was no accident.

I didn't tell my mom about my midlife initiation nose piercing for months, which was made possible by the fact that we lived on separate coasts. Just after my eighteenth birthday, when my mom found out I had secretly pierced my navel, the first sentence she shrieked was, "What will our neighbors think of us at the pool this summer?" Three days later, I had my belly piercing removed. I inherited the belief that appearances matter, so I learned to repress self-expressions that fell outside of social norms. The good girl in me had clamped my whims down all my life. Now I'd had enough of that.

Hours after I got my nose pierced, I picked my daughter up from her summer day camp. She spotted the new piece of jewelry immediately. "That's so cool, Mom, but are you really the type of person who pierces her face?!" Apparently, the domesticated woman she had known me to be thus far would not do such a thing. Though the piercing was a mere pinprick evidencing my fierier parts, it saddened me that I had not, in the decade my daughter had been on Earth, made my fullest self visible to her. I had kept my head down, my heart bound, and my soul cloaked in burp cloths and baggy sweats in those early parenting years. I promised myself that day, right there at the camp pickup spot, to model living with authenticity to both my daughter and my mother as I moved into this second half of my life.

QUEST

If you've picked up this book, it's likely that you're in or near midlife, and you have, at some point or another, found yourself amid your daily life asking: "Is this all there is?" You've probably felt the trembling pangs of "I want more" from somewhere inside. When I entered my forties, I longed for more passion, more depth, more grit, more truth, and more freedom. Perhaps you already know what your personal *more* would look like but just aren't sure how you could possibly go for it. Or maybe you feel the ennui, the loneliness, the burning, but you can't put your finger on what would satisfy it. Either way, I'm willing to bet there are glorious, radiant parts of you (ones you are on the brink of unabashedly claiming!) that no one has ever seen, and they're craving acknowledgement and revelation. I will guide you on this quest of absolute emergence throughout this book. I will do so by telling you my achingly transparent story and by inviting you to get heavy, deep, and real with yourself about your own longing as you cross the threshold into the second half of your life.

LIMINAL

We begin the midlife period when we enter our forties. There, we find ourselves teetering between the first and second half of our lives. In 1950, psychologist Erik Erikson put forth his theory about the stages of psychosocial development. He says that beginning at age forty and lasting until our early sixties, we are presented with a conflict he calls "generativity versus stagnation." This is a period in which we reevaluate our life's purpose to be sure we are making the type of impact on the world that we would like. At this stage, the pull toward growth and generativity became so strong for me that I felt almost allergic to stagnation. For others, the steadiness stagnation offers may feel comfy and familiar. Many fall somewhere in between.

Life's midpoint offers us a shift in perspective from external approval-seeking to internal clarity. We may finally drop all the people-pleasing and focus on what feels most true. We go from having a youthful sense of immortality to the reality of having limited time left. This shift can create a sense of urgency around the changes we are called to make. At this time of life, it is common to feel a gap between the expectations we had for our lives and the reality we are living. We might feel misguided by dreams we've had, exhausted by working and caring for others, and trapped in careers and relationships.

In midlife, when we feel we have hit a plateau in at least one area (career, parenting, etc.), we often find that space is cleared for personal pursuits. This openness can be a welcome (or daunting) invitation to become the authors of our lives—to simplify, differentiate, and deepen into self-possession. This is a time when our quest for purpose can lead us toward a spiritual awakening, giving birth to profound integrity and courageous risk-taking.

In *The Adult Years*, a book from my graduate training that sits on my shelf, Frederic Hudson says, "A great many adults—particularly those who believe they are succeeding—die psychologically at the beginning of the midlife years as they lock themselves out of the incremental gains available in the second half of life. Although their bodies continue to age, their behaviors do not. They remain arrested as persons and do not evolve their stories, plots, or scripts."

In doing qualitative research for this book, I spoke with more than 100 women in their forties. Every single one of them reported they are more enticed by risk, by exploring the unknown, by taking a leap of faith than they ever were at any other age. I acknowledge that it takes a certain level of privilege to move toward that which is still a mystery. As a white, cisgender,[2] neurotypical, relatively affluent person, I have been afforded many privileges I did absolutely nothing to earn. Yes, our system is broken, and not everyone has the luxury of quitting a job or bowing out of the responsibility of various types of relationships. But the plunge needn't be grand. It can be as simple as

---

2   To identify as cisgender is to be a person whose sense of identity and gender corresponds with the sex they were assigned at birth.

taking the next most true step you could possibly take, in each moment.

In the stark light of this midlife intermission, we can do all the things a director starring in her own show does during the break between acts. We can change our costume, edit the dialogue, adjust the music, tweak the lighting, change the set, and switch up the characters in our play. This opportunity to flip the script may feel appealing to some. To others, revisioning the story of our lives can be so paralyzing that we decide to simply use the bathroom and buy some Junior Mints in the lobby until Act Two is underway. Regardless of what we do during this intermission, the curtain will indeed open on the second half. The stage is being set for you to enter, and you get to decide who you want to be.

Historically, the liminal space of this time of life has been called a *midlife crisis*, a term coined in 1965 by psychoanalyst Elliott Jaques. The topic of midlife crisis has been written about ever since, mostly centering the white, male experience. There are various personal-growth books out there for middle-aged women, though I've yet to find one that encourages us to seize the opportunities midlife offers for reclamation and revelation. Based on my experiences of making the raw, inconvenient truth of who I am unapologetically visible in my forties, I know that midlife doesn't need to be an emergency. Let them have their crisis. I much prefer to call this phase of adulthood a *midlife emergence*.

The word *emergence* is defined as "the process of coming into view or becoming exposed after being concealed" or "the process of coming into being, or of becoming important or prominent." Other definitions include phrases like:

"to appear," "to become visible," "to surface," "to arise," "to manifest oneself," "to emanate." The concept of emergence feels resonant with my personal experience of vulnerably unveiling what had previously been unseen.

Making truth visible is a key theme of my life's work. Having been trained as a transpersonal art psychotherapist, I have a graduate degree in making the unconscious conscious. The transpersonal part of my title signifies that I was trained holistically, to consider spirituality as a key component of a person's wellness. It prepared me to incorporate various world wisdom traditions into the practice of mental health instead of relying solely on the mainstream, pathologizing, patriarchal, Western medical models. It normalized my innate pull toward the spiritual and the numinous. The art therapy piece means that during my graduate studies and subsequent therapy practice, I used all forms of art with clients to help give tangible form to their intangible feelings. For example, an art therapy client might draw a tree. Then, when reflecting upon the tree she's drawn, she might identify its deep roots, sheltering branches, and shedding leaves as symbols for her own attributes of being grounded, nurturing, and in transition.

When I began graduate school in 2002, I was most interested in working with adolescents who were undergoing the developmental task of forming their own identities. Jung called this the individuation process: the natural process whereby teenagers separate from, and sometimes rebel against, their caregivers to discover who they truly are as individuals. Looking back, I realize that I was likely drawn to working with this population because I was dissatisfied by my own stunted adolescent individuation process. The first individuation process we go through as teens is an unconscious one. The persona I settled into in that time of my life was an overachieving good girl with a mostly closeted wild side. Growing up as I did, it makes perfect sense that I would assimilate to conventional social roles, play them out, and then make it my career to study them intensely in the first act of my life.

In midlife, we go through a second individuation process. This time, it is more conscious than the first pass at adolescence. It compels us to stand in our center, unswayed by social norms. The stakes are higher, as we are more likely to be settled into longstanding commitments, such as marriages, children, mortgages, or careers. Because of the lives we've created around us by the time we hit our forties, this passage has the potential to be quite disruptive. The second half of life can embolden us to step beyond the boundaries of the conventional identities advocated by our families, social groups, and culture to take the risk of truly becoming ourselves—even if it means seemingly jeopardizing connection, belonging, and acceptance.

MORE

After I gained experience in various therapeutic settings early in my career, I focused my private practice on working with adult women who longed to reclaim the deepest authentic truths during times of great transition, particularly when undergoing the task of individuation. I found that these women ached to reconnect to a juicy vitality and passion they feared they had sacrificed for the sake of careers, children, spouses, or social circles.

As midlife is a natural period of self-reflection, many looked back over their years thus far and pined for the other lives they might have led. The women who came to see me yearned to peel back the adaptive, protective layers of identity they had formed early in life, wishing now to reveal their tender, powerful hearts. So many of my clients were "good girls" in recovery, having done all the "right" things, following our culture's prescription of college to job to marriage to children, only to sit across from me with an unspecified emptiness. Some struggled to find meaning for the time that lies before them. A forty-two-year-old woman recently said to me, "I did have a plan for my life, up until right now."

When our forties begin, we all start to make a shift into midlife. The impetus for this transition can either be via our intentional choices (like deciding to change jobs, leave a marriage, or move to another location) or by way of a situation beyond our control triggering the transformation (such as experiencing the death of a loved one, being laid off, or receiving a medical diagnosis). Regardless of whether the changes we make are voluntary choices or involuntary happenings, the developmental stage of midlife provides us all with an opportunity for radical realignment to our true center. Midlife is a call toward honoring the hard-earned wisdom of our years and using that wisdom to deepen our self-acceptance and self-expression in the sacred time ahead.

When I encounter another human being, especially when in my professional seat as a therapist, guide, or coach, I aim to keep my energetic body positioned with a strong back, an open-hearted front, and wings spread so wide that they can pick up subtle vibrations in the room, like giant, feathery satellite dishes. I soften enough to feel into what is beyond my clients' textured stories. Underneath what is being said, I listen acutely for their soul's longing. Each woman's longing is unique and specific, but the yearning I've heard whispered or shouted most often from the guts of my clients directly into my ears centers on one word:

"Is there more . . . ?"

"I have a hunch there's something more."

"More, please."

"I want more."

"*MORE*!"

More is perhaps the most subversive thing a middle-aged woman can claim. I've been a cheerleader for *more* for hundreds of women, whether they're my family, friends, colleagues, or clients. In our culture, in which women are bred to be quiet, compliant, appreciative, and polite, a woman wanting something beyond what she is given is a radical, patriarchy-shattering act. Fellow therapists know it is no accident who walks into our offices; our clients are so often our mirrors, helping us dive more deeply into our own healing. Once my own fiery, guttural cries for *MORE!* became louder than those of my clients, I paused my private practice and began the inward quest to satisfy all that was unmet in my soul.

That's when I enrolled in that women's circle, and so many other life changes followed. There, in that gorgeous sanctuary in Boulder, the facilitator of that program reflected to me, "Jen, whenever I hear you speak, underneath your words, I just hear your soul crying 'MORE!'" I couldn't help but smile at the resonance.

First, I had to do the hard work of figuring out what exactly was unmet, unseen, and unexpressed. Once I discovered the shape of this yearning within me, I had to summon the courage to make it shamelessly visible. In doing so, I risked my career, my friendships, my connection to my family of origin, and my marriage. But I had to do it anyway, and I had to do it scared, because we only get to live (or at least remember) this one lifetime, and I want to live it out loud and wring it absolutely dry of all the delicious juiciness it offers. I had to own and advocate for my desires each step of the way, painfully facing the guilt and shame they brought up. I turned myself inside out. I broke my own heart only to watch it expand beyond what I thought possible.

PEBBLES

While this is my personal story, I am certainly *not* a heroine in this book. In exposing my most raw, vulnerable places, I fully acknowledge that some of these parts are ugly. I am constantly working on transmuting my gut-churning shame into self-compassion around all the grotesque places. Author and theologian Nadia Bolz-Weber talks about how we are capable of doing the most harm when what we're protecting is the notion that we're good. I do not aim to protect myself in this way. Over time, I've learned not to subscribe to the binary of good and bad. My favorite Rumi quote is printed on a piece of driftwood that sits on my bookshelf: "Out beyond ideas of wrongdoing and rightdoing there is a field. I'll meet you there." This book is my gesture of meeting you in that unprotected field, where I bare my imperfect, messy, human wholeness to normalize and validate it enough for you to do the same.

My story is merely one of many. Yours is, too. Each is like a pebble, dropped into a still pond, sending out reverberating cascades of concentric ripples. We are most affected, impacted, changed where the ripples of our energies collide. When I was in the thick of my marital separation, I posted snippets of my story on social media. Bloop. Ripples. When I spoke about my story on podcasts, more bloops and more ripples. In these cases, I heard back from hundreds of people. The public comments were messages of gratitude for my transparency, support for choosing myself, and respect for facing what I most feared. The private messages I received resounded with, "I thought it was just me!" or, "I want to take a bold step, but I feel trapped," or, "I know we've never met, but can I tell you about my current struggle with this?"

I realized that as a collective, we are famished for truth-telling, thirsty for admitting our confusion to each other. Social media hardly ever breaches daringly honest terrain, instead perpetuating an image of aesthetic perfection, performative self-care, and toxic positivity. Keeping everything neatly inside is such a profoundly lonely way to live. The things that make us feel that alone are actually what have the potential to connect us to one another, if only we felt safe enough to make them visible.

Knowing myself to be a highly sensitive creature impacted by the reactions of others, it is edgy for me to write a book that widely exposes my messy metamorphosis. I've learned that I must tell my story even though I'm afraid, because it's so important to me to say the things

out loud that are often left unsaid. To make the unconscious conscious. To make the unseen seen. To allow my
vulnerability to be a magnet for your own vulnerability. To
be a catalyst for radical truth-telling.

I'm hopeful that letting myself be seen in utter imper-
fection is a reciprocal gift—that being visible is ultimately
healing for me *and* that it frees you up to also be seen
in your most raw state, which becomes healing for you.
I want to invite the often-inconvenient human truth to
come forward in others. I'm more interested in contacting
and loving that place in you (and in me) than I am in anything else in this life.

Just like you, I am a multifaceted being who is flawed,
who is whole, who is holy. Sometimes I long for all parts of
me to be seen and understood, and sometimes I am desperate to hide. I'm tidal, lunar, mutable, human. This is my
attempt to sit beside you and hold your hand while you sign
your own permission slip for *MORE*.

MAP

This book is both a story of my personal path toward claiming more as well as a guide for the rite of passage women
undergo as we enter the second half of our lives. It is my
hope that through hearing the tale of my midlife emergence, you will connect to the unassailable integrity of
whatever is begging to emerge in and through you. Every
chapter of this book unwinds another spiral deeper into
the center of my own midlife journey, and each one culmi-
nates in prompts to guide you into your own self-inquiry
around that topic.

This is not a simple, thirteen-steps-to-freedom-in-your-forties, self-help prescription methodology. Gosh, wouldn't it have been easier on us all if I could have just handed you that book? I cannot, because I know for sure that there is no playbook for midlife other than the one you create for yourself. Each woman's midlife passage will be absolutely unique, with its own quandaries, challenges, and celebrations. As I made my way through my own midlife emergence and guided clients through theirs, I became a cartographer of sorts, pinpointing which signposts proved universal along this developmental journey. I did this so you wouldn't need to walk the path alone.

This book is divided into three parts, across which you'll find thirteen touchstones to visit as you move through your midlife emergence:

Part I: Illumination

The first five chapters are devoted to identifying your unmet, unseen, or unfulfilled longing.

- Chapter 1: The journey begins by feeling into the shape of your own personal cry for *more*.

- Chapter 2: This chapter moves you from stagnation to action by taking the first right step toward what you seek.

- Chapter 3: Here, you will uncover the impressions made by the conditioning you experienced in childhood.

- Chapter 4: This is the time to practice vulnerably making your midlife intentions visible in safe spaces.

- Chapter 5: You will be invited to consciously throw off your personal shackles of domestication by reclaiming your wild.

Part II: Innovation

The middle four chapters are devoted to the intricacies of your unfolding transformation.

- Chapter 6: You'll discover how to cosmically affirm the direction and apex of your soul's calling.

- Chapter 7: You will explore the continuum between safety and risk.

- Chapter 8: You will honor the inward pull, back into a deeper place of quiet realignment with what is most true and essential.

- Chapter 9: This chapter offers a challenge into upleveling by conjuring the courage it takes to make a leap of faith.

Part III: Integration

The final four chapters of this book bring you into a place of integration with the aftermath of your metamorphosis.

- Chapter 10: You will better understand your expansive capacity to hold contrasting emotions at once.

- Chapter 11: This chapter will invite you to work with the emotional reactivity your transition will undoubtedly elicit in others, as well as your response to their reactivity.

- Chapter 12: Here, you'll work with how modeling living by your absolute truth can offer far-reaching healing.

- Chapter 13: The final chapter guides you into creating a vision for your ever-evolving, congruent, powerful future self.

- Continuing to Emerge: You will get a glimpse into how my personal midlife emergence looks and feels six years after it began.

I use the bulk of each chapter to describe my experience of encountering these thirteen themes of the emergence process. Then, each chapter ends with my invitation to you to engage in various activities for your own self-inquiry around that topic. I offer prompts in various modalities, as we all have different styles of processing and making meaning. I include suggestions for journaling, art-making, and personal ceremony. Experiment with the ones you're drawn to or curious about and leave the ones that are not a fit for you. This is intended as a supportive guide to honor your unique, initiatory journey.

May the themes and cues I offer here serve as a brain-storming session for your own personal quest of midlife emergence. May they be a catalyst for unfurling fully into your own authentic identity in the second half of your life.

PART I

illumination

Touching the unmet longing

CHAPTER 1

quaking within

*What would happen if one woman told the truth about
her life?
The world would split open.*

MURIEL RUKEYSER FROM "KÄTHE KOLLWITZ"

OCEAN
June 2017

It was in that summer of the nose piercing when the
tremors of my midlife emergence made themselves
emphatically known. One morning, after inching through
the drop-off car lane at my daughter's summer camp,
instead of heading home, I found myself driving too fast
through the redwood and eucalyptus trees along a snaky,
densely fogged highway that connects San Mateo to Half
Moon Bay. I always slept in as long as I could, so I did the

weekday school and camp drop-off in my pajamas, grateful I did not have to leave the car. On this day, my hair and teeth were still unbrushed. I was braless, wearing a soft gray T-shirt and black sweatpants. As I drove that winding road, the gas pedal carved striped grooves on the ball of my foot and toes; I had left the house in such an emotional haze that morning that I had uncharacteristically forgotten to put on shoes. Though I didn't have a particular destination in mind, I felt like I was hypnotically being pulled toward the ocean. I needed to bring myself to the very edge of something grand.

I used my music playlist as an oracle that morning, clicking the shuffle setting and accepting the songs that came as perfectly timed messengers. The window was halfway down, so the wind whipping by my left ear necessitated turning the volume way up to hear Ani DiFranco sing "So What?" Her song poured through my car's speakers like medicine, not because it eased my pain, but because it so beautifully met it:

> who's gonna give a shit
> who's gonna take the call
> when you find out that the road ahead
> is painted on a wall
> and you're turned up to top volume
> and you're just sitting there in pause
> with your feral little secret
> scratching at you with its claws

The lyrics immediately penetrated my uneasy gut, moved up to my heart like a burning, then got stuck in my throat in a familiar lump. Tears welled up in my eyes, making it hard to see the road. I turned into a state beach parking lot to reorient, my car now facing the Pacific Ocean.

and you're trying hard to figure out
just exactly how you feel
before you end up parked and sobbing
forehead on the steering wheel

who are you now
and who were you then

I stared blankly at the pale gray sky, the dark gray ocean, the flat gray sand. The green, magenta, and yellow portulaca growing between my car and the beach provided the only color. I let my tear-blurred vision find comfort there.

how many times undone
can one person be
as they're careening through the facade
of their favorite fantasy
you just close your eyes slowly
like you're waiting for a kiss
and hope some lowly little power
will pull you out of this.

While sitting salt-water-face to salt-water-face with Momma Ocean, listening to Ani DiFranco croon about her feral little secret, I felt something hot start to crack my inner walls. For the past several months, I had become unbearably restless and inflamed, figuratively and literally, but I feared looking too deeply underneath because it might mean I would have to muster enough bravery to completely change my exquisitely beautiful life. A life where I was so very loved by people who felt like absolute home to me—my husband and daughter. A life that felt as cozy and secure as a blanket fresh from the warm dryer. A life that I was terrified to lose.

In a prayer for courage, I breathed in the ocean air, trying to infuse my being with her powerful, feminine energy. I finally allowed silent sentences to escape the pit in my stomach and burn their way up through my heart and throat until I heard the words finally form in my mind. I whispered my secrets to the ocean because I knew she could hold them until I could set them all free. I confessed to her that it was time to bring forth my lifelong, unfulfilled desire to be in an intimate relationship with a woman.

What was more difficult to (un)swallow was that the particular woman occupying my heart at the time was Emily, my best friend. The friend who lived 1,300 miles away with her wife and their daughter, a family for whom I held deep respect. Emily was the friend who I texted first every morning, last at night, and at least twenty times in between every single day. The friend I studied with and graduated alongside from our master's program at Naropa. The friend I stayed with when I visited Colorado for our shared women's circle that summer. The friend who, one year prior, had slept peacefully through our night of glamping together while I lay awake tormented by a familiar inability to draw a line between friend love and romantic love.

I reached down to turn off the music once the song oracle had delivered its message. There was no turning away from truth now. Seismic waves undulated in my belly that day at the ocean. Magma explodes when it comes into contact with seawater. For what might have been three minutes or three hours, I sat in silence, staring at the sea, bracing for what would happen when I spoke out loud what I knew I needed to speak. Tear-soaked, dirty-haired, wild-eyed, and more awake than I had ever felt, I backed my car out of the parking lot and started down the winding road toward home.

BRACED

One winter evening, when my daughter had just turned six, she and I were having a playful tickle fight on the floor of the living room. She was tickling my neck and smiling expectantly and curiously into my face. I was smiling and giggling a bit and tickling her back, completely entranced by her hearty, rolling laughter. Relentlessly, she kept tickling me and pausing to watch with an evident openness. Then she said, "Mom, let your laugh out! You always seem like you're holding back your true laugh." We paused the tickling, and I asked, "Really? Do I? I feel like I crack up a lot . . . ?" And she said, "No, not like I do. Not like your real, big laugh." In that moment, I felt a deep sadness and an even deeper gratitude for this young, old soul for that earnest reflection.

When our tickle fight picked back up, I laughed, even when it didn't tickle all that much. I found myself laughing to release all the perforated breath that I did so often hold back, a state of holding that my body had become quite familiar with over the years. My daughter watched me laugh with tears forming in her eyes. When a tear eventually fell down her cheek, I said, "Oh, you're crying, sweetie," and she said, "*That's* your real laugh. I never get to see that."

Ever since I was a kid, I had heard infuriating feedback like "lighten up" and "loosen up." As much as I had sought and created a life where I could express myself through art and writing, I felt arrested in how I expressed through my body and my voice. These forms of expression had generally felt stiff and forced. I couldn't remember a time when I felt a sense of ease in my body, in how I moved through the world. During the first half of my life, I continued to carve the deep, well-worn grooves of habitual bracing, clenching, blocking, and silencing my authentic self. Consequently, I would feel angry with myself for showing up as braced or silent, which caused more bracing and silence. It was a cycle I knew very well, and one I became curious to study.

ENERGY

In addition to being a psychotherapist, I've been a Reiki master since my mid-twenties, which means I practice hands-on energy healing work. In doing this work on clients and with myself, I learned how physical patterns in the body can be messengers pointing us toward areas of imbalance. I would be remiss not to pay attention to the fact that my body had been quaking for over twenty years, letting me know I was not living in alignment with the shape my soul was meant to take.

In 2005, I wrote my master's thesis on how psychotherapists could use the chakra system as a diagnostic tool for their clients; it seemed more holistic and strengths-based than the Diagnostic and Statistical Manual of Mental Disorders (DSM), the authoritative guide to the diagnosis of mental health issues that has been met with criticism since its inception for over-diagnosing and for pathologizing normal emotional responses. In studying the chakra system, I learned that the chakras are spheres of bioenergetic activity emanating from nerve ganglia, the seven major ones stacked along the spinal column. Each of the major chakras is related to an area of the body, to various psychological issues, and to developmental skills. I had been fascinated by the chakra system since middle school, and I had later applied this knowledge in my work. However, it became valuable to me personally since I spent my twenties and thirties suffering from various physical discomforts and mostly invisible mystery illnesses. I was eager to discover where these imbalances originated so I could address the root of the issues and finally move toward healing.

INFLAMED

I had endured debilitating chronic pain since I was about twenty-five years old, particularly in the form of severe knee inflammation. *Inflammation* literally means that there is an inner fire. (Clearly!) For decades, I had suffered cyclical bouts of intense knee swelling lasting for three out of every eleven days. I would wake up on the first day of the cycle with swollen balloons for knees. On what my family began to call "knee days," I had a very difficult time getting up and down, walking for long distances, or doing any sort of exercise. I attempted to schedule my activities and commitments so they wouldn't fall on "knee days." After countless doctors and healers tried to treat this condition over the decades (to no avail), I found a wonderful functional medicine practitioner who was able to trace this odd occurrence to dormant (stage four) Epstein-Barr virus that was overburdening my sensitive system—all because I had mononucleosis in ninth grade from sharing Big Gulps with my cheerleading squad. The small decision I made to drink from a communal Dr. Pepper at halftime during a basketball game when I was thirteen had a monumental impact on my life.

This particular internal fire had taken up residence in my vulnerable knees, as they had been weakened by a medical intervention that happened before I had even learned to walk. In the mid-1970s, it was common to misdiagnose children as "pigeon-toed" if their feet turned in when they lay on their backs, though pediatricians now know one cannot make such a diagnosis until a child is actually walking. As I was first learning to propel my body through space via crawling and walking, I spent eighteen hours a day wearing these little white leather shoes that curved outward like two crescent moons, attached by a thick brass bar between them.

In my chakra studies, I discovered that the second chakra had been developing while I was wearing that brace. This chakra governs sexuality, emotions, creativity, desire, boundaries, and movement. When I was Nancy Drew-ing my way to figuring out why I had spent twenty years limping around, an osteopath explained to me that because my tibia had grown spiraled and torqued in that unnecessary brace, my knees had become a vulnerable spot where inflammation could settle. When I was a baby, my parents thought they were doing what was best for my future, but I've since learned that there was virtually no chance I would have become pigeon-toed, so I didn't even need that brace.

Braced when I was learning about moving my body and exploring my world. Braced when I was psychologically learning how to set healthy boundaries, while being more bound than I naturally would have been. Braced when the chakra governing sexuality and sensuality was awakening.

This formative, preverbal developmental period has a profound impact on each of us. For me, it began my pattern of keeping myself braced tightly, inhibited from trusting my body to handle new explorations or open sexual expression.

VOICE

The second chakra bracing came first, and then came the fifth chakra clenching and silencing, as these two chakras are often in direct relationship to one another. The fifth chakra resides in the throat and governs communication and the act of speaking one's truth. Mine could be categorized as deficient. This imbalance points to the fact that in this body, in this life, I experienced troubles during this chakra's developmental period (ages seven to twelve) that caused me to be fearful of speaking up and somewhat shy about putting my voice out there. Circumstances that can affect fifth chakra development include authoritative parents, excessive criticism, abusive/addictive family patterns, and mixed messages. When I read the books on how this can manifest physically in the body, I checked the boxes beside almost every symptom: hypothyroidism (check!), TMJ-D or Temporomandibular Joint Dysfunction (check!), a weakened/raspy voice and susceptibility to laryngitis (check!), and a tongue tie (check!)

A person with TMJ-D generally clenches their jaw in their sleep like they are holding on for dear life. TMJ-D is a condition we pick up by observing our parents and learning how to hold stress—my mom has it, too. It can be amplified by anxiety. My symptoms began when I was twenty years old. In my sleep, I tried to use the immense power of my jaw to hold tightly to something. Even when I was unconscious, it was difficult for me to let go.

I also had notable bouts of complete laryngitis during significant moments in my life. Interestingly, most were pivotal moments at the start of something that stifled a bigger part of my truth. I found myself voiceless:

- The week I rushed a sorority that I eventually quit because the group's values were at odds with my own.

- My first day working in New York City at a job where I eventually became financially successful while compromising my health, my passion, and my soul.

- The day I met Craig, who would become my dear husband for seventeen years, while I paused the full expression of my sexuality.

- On my and Craig's wedding night and for most of our honeymoon.

- The afternoon I told my best friends that I had a crush on Emily.

- The day Craig and I decided to purchase our "forever home," which turned out not to be forever.

I was also born with a bit of a tongue tie. This means that the little fleshy part under my tongue that connects it to the floor of my mouth (the lingual frenum) was unusually tight at birth, restricting my tongue's range of motion. It also affected the way I ate, spoke, and swallowed. I didn't discover this until I entered my forties, and it ended up playing quite a role in my midlife emergence.

VISION

While the energies of my second and fifth chakras ran low, my sixth chakra had always been on overdrive. The sixth chakra is also known as the third eye and is located on the brow. This energy center governs vision and intuition, and it awakens at the stage of life when the developmental task is to establish a personal identity. My excessive sixth chakra energy had manifested as headaches and vision problems in the form of light sensitivity, floaters, headaches, migraines, auras, and brain fog. I have found it interesting that this chakra develops during adolescence, when we are first individuating from our families and defining our identities. This type of awakening happens again during midlife, when the roles we previously adopted may no longer satisfy. We can find ourselves cast into the fertile darkness, and if we are able to see clearly through the dark, through whatever clouds our vision, we have an opportunity to reemerge with what has the potential to be a spiritual awakening.

In the past several years, I've been praying for clarity in that murky darkness—the type of insight that would allow me to see clearly. In making major life decisions, I've had to strip away all external messages, advice, and opinions to look deep inside. It's been difficult to get to the unadulterated vision—to find something pure enough that I know it comes directly from within myself. And to listen to it, and follow it, and speak it, and act upon it. This is the work of a seer.

MESSENGERS

On that foggy day when I was parked along the Pacific Ocean, I finally saw with clarity. I heard the inner call, loud and clear. The volume knob got turned all the way up until I could no longer deny the scream inside my body, mind, and heart that I needed to commit to radical integrity to fully emerge as my most authentic and free self. I knew I would have to give up so much to court who I was truly becoming, even if she still felt like a nebulous mystery. There was no map for the territory I was about to traverse.

In hindsight, I understand that my body had been communicating her imbalances for years, gifting me with emotional and physical signs of misalignment. Regardless of her patterns of bracing, clenching, muting, and fogging up, the potent message of my truth broke through all the barriers I had unconsciously built against it. As much as I shamed myself for not appreciating the enoughness of my life, the internal voice wondering *"Is this all there is?"* persistently, painfully, and passionately returned. I now consider every one of my symptoms to be blessings, pointing me toward the pieces of myself I had yet to grow.

After years of being bound, my own personal experience of the midlife passage included the yearning for boundless, raucous self-expression. Longing is the soul's way of calling itself back home, over and over again. Let's amplify the call of our souls to a level where we can hear them, and at least take baby steps toward living our lives to their most expansive potential.

WRITE

You may wish to find a dedicated journal or notebook for the writing prompts in this book. Or you can grab a journal you're already using, open a new document on your computer to type your responses, or simply jot your writing on scrap paper. You don't need to be precious about it. Let it be easy.

Here's your first set of writing prompts:

- You know that thing you've been secretly mulling over? Maybe it's a relationship. A job. A move. A creation. A beginning. An ending. A longing. . . . Call it up in your gut, your mind, your heart.

- Be still. Listen inwardly. What are the words you hear being whispered? Or maybe yours are being shouted. Write them down. Even if you have to write them in light pencil or invisible ink today, or even if you have to burn the paper after—write them anyway.

- What is the feeling arising just beneath or behind those words? Do you feel any sensations in your body? Have you noticed any symptoms in your throat? Your belly? The base of your spine? Describe what you feel.

- What is the one sentence you are most afraid to say to others? To yourself? Write it down. Say it out loud.

- Dig deeper. What aren't you saying, even still? What aren't you writing down? That is what is longing to be unearthed in midlife. (Pssst: You already know.)

CREATE

Grab a blank piece of paper and a writing implement. It's a bonus if you happen to have a set of colored pencils, crayons, or other colorful drawing materials handy.

First, draw a simple outline of your body, head to toe, preferably as a hollow-contour drawing, simply showing a human shape. Now, close your eyes and sit in mindful silence for three minutes. Turn your attention inward to observe the landscape of your body. Which parts feel comfort or pleasure, which feel neutral, and which feel discomfort or pain? Notice if any part has a message to share, whether it's a color, a word, or a phrase.

When you open your eyes, place lines, shapes, colors, words, and/or phrases on the human figure you drew. Maybe the chest area felt like a red-hot comet, screaming the word "Love!" Perhaps the legs ache with blue longing. Maybe you envision spiritual connection as a warm, yellow glow radiating from your head. Consider this a visual map of what your body is saying—it often knows your secrets well before your mind gets the message, and art has a way of communicating directly from our unconscious, without filters.

ALTAR RITUAL

You are cordially invited to create a physical space where you will tend to your personal process as you move through this book. I like to call mine an altar and will refer to it as an altar throughout this book, but you may name it as you wish. This altar will be dedicated to honoring your own midlife emergence. An altar is the resting place for your inner divinity. This new altar is a location where you can focus on the idea that you are growing into your higher self in the second half of life. You're welcome to add to it with each chapter's theme or clear it off between chapters and start anew as you move to another phase.

First, simply locate a space in your home that you can devote to yourself. It could be a small table, a shelf, a corner, a space on your dresser or nightstand, a windowsill, the edge of your bathtub, a sheltered spot in your garden. Choose a spot that feels private enough for you to hold as sacred.

Clear it off completely. Dust it. Clean it. If you're someone who is into smoke cleansing, raid your spice cabinet and let the smoke of a burning bay leaf rid this spot of old energy, or allow the smoke from burning dried rosemary to invite in new energy. Mindfully prepare the area as a holding space for this journey you are embarking upon.

Next, find or purchase a candle for your altar. This flame will signify the inner voice, the inner fire, the inner longing. Place it at the center of your altar and light it.

Sit or stand quietly in front of your new altar. Read (to yourself or out loud) what you wrote for the prompts above to infuse this sacred space with the intention for your quest.

CHAPTER 2

launching
softly

*Truth is not fully explosive, but purely
electric. You don't blow the world up with
the truth; you shock it into motion.*

CRISS JAMI *HEALOLOGY*

KISS

On that gray morning when I was staring at the ocean
through blurry, wet eyes, I admitted to myself that I loved
Emily in a way I could not ignore. Once I had heard my
inner voice so clearly, I knew I couldn't just let it echo
within my own heart chambers. I had to take action to
make my insides congruent with how I was living my life
on the outside. There was a lasting truth deep within that
was making an urgent plea to be exposed.

I remember watching *Who's the Boss* as a kid and
trying to decide whether I wanted to *be* Alyssa Milano or

if I wanted to *kiss* her. Nearly every intimate or sexual fantasy I've had in my life has centered around, or at least included, a woman. Throughout grade school and early adulthood, I had had crushes on probably a dozen female friends with whom I had deep connections. Through these real-life crushes, I discovered that the emotional bond needed to be strong for me to feel attraction toward someone, an identity that's known as demisexual.[1] The types of emotional relationships I experienced with girls (and now women) fostered attraction more easily than the connections I had made with boys or men. Yet, I found myself exclusively in romantic relationships with men up to and including my marriage.

I grew up in a conservative environment in the South. As a teenager with very little exposure to or modeling of acceptance around queer relationships, I didn't talk with my friends about my attraction to women. I wasn't even aware that queer relationships were an option. I was years away from a time—and states away from a place—where queer love was sanctioned.

Even so, my first kiss was with a girl. We were in the fifth grade, riding in the backseat of her parents' boxy, champagne-colored Buick on the way back to her house for a sleepover. We had just had dinner at some chain restaurant on the outskirts of the mall. "Every Breath You Take"

---

1   Demisexuality is a sexual orientation in which someone feels sexual attraction only to people with whom they have an emotional bond. From https://demisexuality.org/articles/what-is-demisexuality/

by The Police was playing on the radio. I remember lying down together across the leather seats, looking up at the streetlights as we rode in the dark, singing along with Sting. Suddenly, she was on top of me, kissing me with full-on tongue for the duration of the song, unbeknownst to her parents. It felt soft and electric. Once we were back at her house and ready for bed, I desperately wanted her to kiss me again, but she didn't. I was too stunned and shy to initiate, so I rolled over and tried to sleep through the buzzing in my brain and body. I stayed awake half the night.

Despite the memory of this experience being etched into the cells of my lips and tongue, whenever asked about my first kiss, I've always said it happened with my first serious boyfriend, Jim, on the beach one night in November of ninth grade. I didn't say this to hide the moment in the backseat of the car years before. I honestly just did not consider the kiss with a girl as a first kiss; I had zero frame of reference for queer intimacy.

Jim and I dated for five years, beginning the night of that kiss on the beach. During those turbulent teenage years, he and I grew up together. We talked on the phone late into each night about our existential teen crises, we fought terribly, we cheated on each other, and we sweetly made up a zillion times. In that relationship, I was madly in love, devastatingly heartbroken, and everything in between—each emotion visceral and real to my adolescent heart.

At twenty-two, after a particularly heart-wrenching end to an almost four-year relationship with another man, I developed an intense crush on a very close girlfriend of mine. I was too timid to ever tell her about it for fear that it would ruin our friendship. I had confided in a few other friends who tried to encourage me to open up to her. Instead, I ran away from the complexity telling her would have produced. In the grief of the break up and the confusion over the crush on my friend, I wanted to start over. I moved from Virginia to New York City, and I vowed to myself that it was time to explore this part of my sexuality and finally find a proper girlfriend.

DISMISSED

When I moved to New York in the late nineties, I became a successful cog in the early dot-com machine. One of the pivotal times in my life when I had complete laryngitis was on the first day at my new job at a prominent internet advertising company. My boss showed me to my desk: a low-walled cubicle in a sea of other cubicles cluttering a large, warehouse-type space, a trend in the tech world at that time. I could only wave and mouth "Hello," as I was introduced to the other most recent hire, Craig, whose desk was directly in front of mine. I noticed two things about him that day: he had a warm smile and a coffee mug with Animal from the Muppets on it (my childhood favorite). In that first week of the job, he walked by my computer screen and saw that I played Ani DiFranco in my headphones as I worked. He was also a fan. Craig and I quickly became friends, having lunches together at the diner across from our office and going out most nights to explore our new city and to admire beautiful women together.

Craig knew from the jump that I desired to be with women, similar to a few bisexual women he dated before me. Almost four months after we met, we began dating. Even then, he said he would be okay with my being with a woman sexually. However, at that age, I held myself and my partners to a standard of strict monogamy. Having been scarred by cheating and being cheated on, I no longer acted on impulses that would take me outside of my relationship. Three years into dating, Craig and I got engaged, and we eventually had a large wedding in my hometown in June 2003. Amidst the flurry of bridesmaid activity in the back room of my parents' country club, preparing to walk down the aisle, I watched the bridesmaid I had been crushing on five years before apply her lipgloss in our shared mirror. Under my simple, white dress, I felt the smallest quiver of my sinking heart, acknowledging my unmet desire for being in a romantic relationship with a woman. Simultaneously, my heart also beamed the purest love toward the wonderful man awaiting me at the altar. Hearts are amazing multitaskers.

By the time I had met Craig at twenty-three, I would talk with almost anyone about my sexuality if they asked. In my adult life, I had never felt closeted about my attraction to women, but I rarely brought it up or made it overt. Even though it felt like a big part of me, I just wasn't sure where it fit. It hardly came up in conversation because I was in a relationship with a man, which was enough evidence for most people to check the "hetero" box for me. Generation X may be the last generation to have succumbed to compulsory heterosexuality (often shortened to comphet), a theory Adrienne Rich popularized in the 1980s stating that a patriarchal society expects and enforces heterosexuality. I think of comphet as assuming everyone is straight until they say otherwise, and I experienced it as a child with adults around me saying things like "Do you have a little boyfriend, sweetheart?" or the bizarre compliment that "Boys will be knocking down the door to date you when you grow up!"

I often felt a childish pout of injustice over not being seen in the fullness of my sexuality. For example, sometimes when I saw two women kissing in a movie theater or walking hand-in-hand in a park, I felt a suffocating mixture of grief, anger, and envy. I resented their freedom, and I believed I was too far down another path and too arrested by commitments to act upon the pull deep inside me. While I was aware of my queerness even before I had a frame of reference for it, my desire to experience and express it only increased as I aged.

I vividly remember the first time I told my mom I was bisexual, which, in my early twenties, was the language I used to describe my sexuality. Because I did not yet have the resources or support to understand comphet culture, how else was I to explain that I was dating men *and* attracted to women? My mom had spent the weekend visiting me in New York City, and we had just finished packing up her suitcase on a Sunday morning. We were sitting by the front bay window in the brownstone apartment Craig and I shared in Park Slope, Brooklyn, just before we got engaged. During a light conversation about attractive people, I admitted to my mom that I was attracted to women. I said it in a way that I initially thought was cool and casual, but upon hearing the words come out of my mouth and hang in the air, my heart beat bright red across my cheeks as I awaited her response. Distractedly looking out the window for the car that would soon take her to LaGuardia Airport, she said, "Well, you're lucky you found Craig!" I was crestfallen. In addition to casual mentions, I intentionally brought it up with her again at least five more times over the next two decades, and each time was met with a similar reply. Hearing my sexuality dismissed by my mom always felt to me, internally, like another (weighty) vote that I should put those pieces of myself away. So I did. I buried them under my flushed skin, over and over again.

IDENTITY

For twenty more years, the flame of my unmet longing grew hotter. Once I hit forty, the invisibility of my queerness burned inside in ways that felt toxic, damaging—sickening, even. Social worker Sula Malina says that queer invisibility is a function of biphobia (the prejudice against bisexual people) and monosexism (the belief that everyone should be attracted to one gender). Psychologically, when we are not acknowledged for our sexual or gender identities, it has the potential to lead to a sense of disconnection from the self and a whole host of mental-health issues. Others' false projections can be incredibly damaging. By being in a marriage with a cis man, most people assumed I was heterosexual, or felt that my sexuality was not an issue because of my relationship status. Rather than "coming out" over and over again, I simply stopped correcting assumptions.

I am relieved that the rising social consciousness aims to shatter antiquated, binary gender assumptions that are ignorantly based on biological sex, appearance, or romantic partners. Society has historically failed at educating us around the difference between sex and gender, though Generation Z is thankfully making strides toward changing this. As I write this in the early 2020s, people are still throwing "gender-reveal parties" for unborn babies, releasing either pink or blue balloons, when really all they can possibly reveal is the shape of the genitals attached to the human growing inside their mother.

Sex, or assigned sex, is a label given at birth based on genitals, hormones, and chromosomes. Most people are assigned male or female, and if the anatomy doesn't fit into either, they may be described as intersex.

Gender does not always align with assigned sex. Binary gender roles are social constructs around behaviors, thoughts, and characteristics that go along with being a girl or a boy, a woman or a man. Our gender identity is where we feel most aligned. If one's gender feels aligned with the sex they were assigned at birth, they are said to be cisgender. People whose gender does not align with their assigned sex can fall along a spectrum that lives under the transgender umbrella, which includes both binary trans folks and non-binary/gender-nonconforming folks. Gender identity (cisgender, transgender, gender-nonconforming, etc.) is *not* the same as gender expression (feminine, androgynous, masculine, etc.), which is *not* the same as biological sex (female, intersex, male), which is *not* the same as sexual orientation (heterosexual, bisexual, queer, fluid, homosexual, etc.).

Sexuality is not defined by gender presentation or appearance. As a cisgender woman, I am often assumed to be straight because I am perceived in a way our culture has defined as "feminine." Given this, I've become all too familiar with *queer femme invisibility*. I consider myself *femme* because the word femme denotes the queering of the construct of femininity. Femme is a reclamation of agency over how I physically present, intersecting with my sexuality. For me personally, being femme is a combination of soft and strong, tender and fierce. I may enjoy wearing a little makeup, but adding a harder edge to my inherent softness makes me feel powerful. I wear combat boots with my dresses and a smoky, woody essential-oil blend in my long, wavy hair. That's when I feel most like myself—most fully expressed and confident.

Sexuality also cannot be defined by the gender of a person's romantic partner. Even when I was sleeping with men, I was absolutely queer. I am overtly aware of the privilege I had in walking hand-in-hand with Craig in public for over twenty years, in that I was not an immediate target for violence and harassment because my queerness was cloaked. I'm certainly not asleep or immune to the reality of marginalization, discrimination, and violence inflicted upon the queer community. However, on the other side of this privilege is the pain of invisibility. My sexuality had been largely hidden during my years of being in a straight-passing marriage and presenting as what is considered feminine. I've felt misunderstood and frustrated in this realm for much of my life. Our culture is quick to conflate partners and gender presentation with sexual identity.

This is such a spirited time in our world—full of potential in the ways people are moved to take action for inclusion and equity. It's my personal and political (they are the same, really) hope that we open our hearts and minds to gain a broader understanding of intersectionality and all parts of our multifaceted identities. Like any person, I long to be seen, heard, and known in the full truth of my being.

COUNCIL

Grown out of my processing of the invisibility wound, radical truth-telling became a priority in my life, personally and professionally. Council is a practice I have engaged in with several circles of therapists, healers, and spiritual practitioners. The tradition of council comes from various ancient world wisdom traditions and was developed thousands of years ago. I personally learned about it through the lineage of depth psychologist Bill Plotkin's nature-based, soul initiation work. In council, there is a talking piece of some sort, like a stone or a stick, or anything nearby. The person who holds it is the only one who speaks. There are only four rules in council: for the speaker to speak from the heart, for the listener(s) to listen with the ears of the heart, for the speaker to get to the heart of the matter without many tangents, and for the speaker to be spontaneous in not preparing what they might share. The purpose is to let what arises in the speaker to be witnessed in the sacred container of a circle of people or in the dyad of a relationship. Sometimes, the listener(s) will have a chance to reflect to the speaker the impact of what they have heard, without advising, fixing, or sharing their own related story. Then the talking piece is passed to another participant who takes their turn speaking their own truth. This form of mirroring allows the speaker's story to be received and honored. Craig and I sometimes held our own private council at home, just the two of us, when we needed to work through heavy emotional material.

The last time we held council at home was a few weeks before my forty-first birthday, when I came to him to discuss my wish for us to be more open, raw, and real with one another. I was feeling a desire to break all the patterns we had lazily fallen into around parenting, household responsibilities, money, jealousy, and sex. To signify this shift, we even picked out a new wedding ring for me to wear. My old one held a large solitaire diamond (passed down from his mom) in a pristine platinum setting; the new one reflected the current energy of our union—a golden setting supporting an earthy, irregular, imperfect, raw diamond with a tiny, white diamond (representing our daughter) nestled beside it.

CONFESSION

After that momentous drive to the beach on that June morning, my truth was right at the surface. I longed to share its details with the person closest to me in the world. So, on that very same night, I asked Craig if we could hold council after our daughter was asleep. Once we had tucked her in together, we sat in the living room on opposite couches. I told him about my time on the coast that morning. I confessed that my sexual energy was returning full force, and that it was solely tethered to the idea of being with a woman. I let him know that I was currently preoccupied and distressed about my attraction toward Emily. He listened so attentively and with such empathy.

When it was his turn to respond, he said, "I knew you were queer when I married you. This was bound to come up, and here it is, and it's all okay, babe. You're not alone in it. We'll figure it out together." Craig was never threatened by the fact that I was attracted to women. That night, he told me that he was still open to my being with a woman sexually, as long as it did not change the way I ultimately felt about him. He understood the gravity of this persistent desire and knew I couldn't keep this piece of myself at bay any longer. That night was when we first discussed the idea of engaging in ethical non-monogamy, when all parties consent to a sexual or romantic relationship that involves more than two people.

In that conversation, I could not reciprocate his generous openness in that I couldn't bring myself to say I felt comfortable with him also being with another woman. My jealousy wound was old and deep, and something I was willing to work on healing by venturing slowly into open marriage. Craig said he would not be okay with my being with another man (which had never appealed to me, anyway). Interestingly, even though we knew this was a limited, archaic view, we both felt threatened about our spouse engaging in sex with someone who, in outdated binary terms, identified as the same gender as we did. This was perhaps due to our early conditioning and wounds that had yet to heal. We left that evening's council with the agreement that I was welcome to explore sexually with women. He said he felt satisfied with that for the time being, but we both acknowledged that, in time, reciprocity was perhaps something to work toward, as this imbalance could foster resentment. All of it felt like risky territory, but it released some of the pressure that had built inside me.

I went to sleep that night with deep gratitude and appreciation for our bond, in being granted the freedom to engage with the energy that was begging to unfold. He loved me enough to support me in being the freest version of myself. He gave his blessing for me to expand the capacity of my heart to include Emily or other women, and for me to be able to act on my attractions. I did not wish to blow up my wonderful life and my loving marriage, but I knew I had to live more congruently, more visibly, and more in partnership with this inner fire that felt both sacred and taboo. I fell asleep beside him, feeling deeply safe and unconditionally loved.

HOMESICK

One night, just a few weeks after that council, I had just returned from my monthly trip to Colorado. I physically ached over how much I missed Colorado and how profoundly lonely I felt in California. Craig and I had lived in Boulder during my graduate-school years, during which we had gotten married. My personal, professional, and spiritual community continued to reside in and around the Boulder area. As a family, we three visited often for weddings, births of babies, friends' birthdays, and simply for social contact. I took several solo professional and social trips to Boulder over the years, too, always to find myself gutted at the Denver airport, boarding my flight back to California. In all these trips, it's probable that I baptized every concourse at the Denver airport with my tears.

Flying from a place that felt like home to a place where I had not been able to put down roots or find my people caused great dissonance in my body and soul. Craig and I had always acknowledged that someday we would likely return to Boulder, though we weren't sure when.

We moved to the San Francisco Bay Area during the financial crash of 2009 so that Craig's tech career could keep us afloat. While I was able to start my private psychotherapy practice in California, I felt unsatisfied in my professional community. I made a few solid friends over the years, but nothing could compare to the delight of the group of deep friendships I maintained 1,300 miles away. The cost of living in the Bay Area prohibited us from buying a home there, and I felt we were throwing money away on overpriced, outdated rentals with Pepto-Bismol-pink-tiled bathrooms. Craig loved living in the Bay Area, being on the cutting edge of what was happening in the tech world, enjoying perfect weather, and having access to so much clean food and gorgeous road-tripping destinations. Now that Craig was well established in his industry, he could essentially work from anywhere. Regardless, he preferred to stay there, on that palm-treed peninsula.

That night, as I cried in bed after my trip, heartsick and homesick for Boulder, we stayed awake all night talking about location and happiness and money and community. By morning, we had decided that in one year, we would make the move to Boulder. Over that year, Craig would secure his position so that the move would be professionally viable, and we would research schools and purchase a home in our favorite foothills. The timing felt right, as the move would occur the summer between our daughter's elementary school and middle school years, allowing a smoother transition for her. The decision to move was a mutual one, though we both knew it was for my well-being. We had moved from New York to Boulder for my career in 2002, then in 2009 to California for his career, and now it was my turn again. I expressed a need, and we found a way to meet it. Though this sort of compromise is a feature of most healthy relationships, my excitement about the changes ahead was tinged with guilt and selfishness. Craig voiced that he was afraid he might lose me to someone else once we moved to a place where I had such promise of true connections, and I was adamant that he would never, ever lose me.

Over the course of that final year in California, Craig and I continued to make efforts to update our relationship and expand into forms of higher love for one another. Venturing into this brand-new territory felt both scary and hopeful. We certainly did not jump into anything quickly or blindly, knowing that all we needed to do was take the next right step, and to do so in integrity, in the light, and in loving communication. We read all the books we could find on ethical non-monogamy, from *More Than Two* to *Opening Up* to *The Ethical Slut*. We held council almost weekly to process our feelings about our pending move to Boulder and into polyamory. We eventually began to see a couples counselor who specialized in open relationships. We attended talks on ethical non-monogamy, perused dating apps together, and kept our dialogue on the topic open and respectful. I was so grateful not to be rolling this around in my head all alone any longer.

EXPRESS

With all the heat and pressure that had built up inside, I needed to express—which literally means to press out—what I had been holding onto so tightly. For me, truth-telling began by talking with Craig—the safest, most supportive, most loving person I have been honored to know in this lifetime. As soon as I spoke the words, I felt freer. He helped hold my truth alongside me, and he reflected back to me its validity and importance. This made me wonder why I had held it in for so long.

What keeps us hiding our deliciously awkward truths from each other? I think it's the stigma around anything that looks messy, the shame in the untamed, and, at our deepest core, the fear of not being loved. The irony is, I have repeatedly seen evidence of being loved, accepted, and welcomed more fully when we are our most soft, unguarded, and unmasked selves.

I had no idea what it would look like on the other side of this passage. I did not have a clear vision in my mind's eye. I remember my therapist suggesting I trust-fall off the cliff, into the dark unknown. At the time, that bold idea paralyzed me completely. When I felt into what was right for me, all I could do was take the next right step. Just one. I took a breath and vowed not to get too far ahead of myself, as the map for my path was materializing in real time, under my footfall.

At that point, I had done the work of listening deeply to what needed to shift in each area of my life. I admitted to myself that I wanted to experience a different type of intimacy. I paused my private practice, not knowing what the next iteration of my career would be. I prepared to move my family to Boulder, not knowing any of our fates in this new place. I confessed to Craig my longing to be in a relationship with a woman, not knowing how that could manifest or what it might do to our marriage. In mustering the courage to make these bold moves, I learned that the freedom we seek lives on the other side of the conversations we avoid.

WRITE

What's the very first bite-sized, doable step in your course of action toward absolute self-alignment? Trust your intuition here. It could be a conversation you need to have, a trip you need to book, a change you need to make in your schedule, or some other catalyst that shifts potential, inward energy into kinetic, outward energy.

Brainstorm in writing how you can begin to create movement toward the shift that's begging to be made. Make a plan for yourself. Set a date for when you will take the first right step toward your true self. Put it on your calendar. If it is something you can do today, in this moment, take a deep breath, exhale it all out, take action.

CREATE

To inspire the first baby step toward your future, take a walk in your neighborhood or city, or in a nearby natural environment like a forest, beach, mountain, or any place that you have easy access and calls to you. This will be an exercise in *kairomancy*, a term coined by Australian author and historian Robert Moss. It means "divination by special moments or meaningful coincidences." A kairomancer is one who is guided by little synchronicities and is ready to seize the opportunity they present. In this practice, you will use the phenomena that arise as guidance for what to do next, like a walking oracle or a conscious dream.

When you move through your environment with open awareness, you'll notice that the world is consistently sending you messages in the form of signs and symbols. Let yourself be guided by the relationship between your inner voice and the world around you. Maybe you'll get curious about a signpost and go where it leads. Perhaps you'll follow the path of a scampering squirrel or go in the direction of a bird flying overhead. Maybe you'll hear children playing in the distance or a song coming out of a car window that gives you a clue about your next step. This practice helps you tune into your intuition and the guidance that always surrounds you.

Collect one object from your kairomancy walk that reminds you of living in sync with the universe. It could be a rock, shell, leaf, feather, or a curious found object. It could be a photo you took of a mural in an alley. Feel free to paint or write words on it, if that's possible, reflecting your feelings about taking a first step. You may choose to place this object on your midlife emergence altar.

ALTAR RITUAL

On a small piece of paper, write the first step you will take and the date you will take it. Kiss it. Put the slip of paper under the candle on your altar then light the candle.

If you've already done the first step, sit at your altar in recognition and appreciation of your own courage. Congratulate yourself for setting into motion whatever it is that will help you feel your freest.

If you have not yet taken the first step, while sitting at your altar, apply a little reverse-perspective magic here. Hold the idea in your heart that this first step is already done, it has already happened, and it went beautifully. Your palms may have been sweaty, your heart may have been racing, your voice may have been shaking, but you did it. You are becoming more *you*. Hold that vision in your mind as you invoke the courage needed to do the next right thing. (You got this!)

CHAPTER 3

illuminating
early conditioning

*[Articulate] exactly how you don't belong,
the exact dimensionality of your exile . . .
and you're on your way home.*

DAVID WHYTE
FROM *ON BELONGING & COMING HOME*, YOUTUBE TALK

INTROJECTS

As my white-hot truth quaked underground in my early forties, I couldn't help but wonder how I, someone who had devoted much of my adult life to self-inquiry work in becoming a psychotherapist, had gotten to a place of self-abandonment. Our truth can often be mysterious, even to our own psyche. Sometimes, our deepest longing is so shrouded in layers of conditioning and conformity that it is hard to clearly see and name who we are and what we want. I began to look at the first half of my life to examine external messages from society and family that had formed the person I had become. In psychology, these ideas and attitudes we unconsciously adopt from others are known as *introjects*.

In our formative years, even beginning in the womb, each of us absorbed introjects about topics such as needs, sex, power, love, expression, spirituality, and more. Every family system has its own rules of operating, whether spoken or unspoken, conscious or unconscious. Often, these guidelines for living are passed down through generations, through both nature and nurture. The study of epigenetics has shown that our DNA can be changed in response to the environment in which we are living, and this DNA can pass down the emotional legacy of trauma, anxiety, and depression. Therefore, we are capable of feeling the impact of experiences going back two or three generations, and generations after ours could inherit our emotional blueprint.[1]

As a parent, I understand firsthand how much we want our children to feel safe—it's instinctual. To continue down a familiar, well-grooved path inherently feels like the most secure way to rear a child. There is a lot of momentum (generally based in fear) behind maintaining familial norms, so it takes fortitude to deviate, even in the smallest acts.

As a white, middle-class female born in 1975 in southeastern Virginia, the air I grew up breathing was heavy with

---

1   From Mark Wolynn, *It Didn't Start With You* (New York: Penguin Publishing Group, 2016).

stenches of sexism, racism, and homophobia; a desperate grip on monogamy; sexual modesty bordering on repression; blind trust in authority and experts; a scarcity-based work ethic; martyrdom as prized in motherhood—all with a waft of pseudo-Christianity breezing about. These were the undercurrents of the time and place and people from which I came. These were values my family lineage had deemed secure and familiar for generations, so I was brought up under those conditions to keep me as safe as my parents knew how. As I work my ass (and ego) off to understand and uproot my own introjects, I also bow deeply to each person in my lineage. I am grateful to them for being the life rafts they have been—loving me, caring for me, and getting me to where I am today in the best way they knew how.

NEEDS

I grew up in a household of tremendous care and good intentions, underneath a cloud filled with expectations, obligations, and unspoken rules. In writing on what she calls "the mother wound," Bethany Webster says, ". . . for daughters growing up in a patriarchal culture, there is a sense of having to choose between being empowered and being loved." Like many of us, I was born into a time and a family where I had to choose between these two. From the time my tiny and supremely permeable being could pick up on energy, I surmised that being an "easy baby" and a "good girl" were prized over expressing genuine needs.

When I was a smiling, quiet baby, I was rewarded. When I did what babies naturally do to communicate their preverbal needs—have a tantrum or a breakdown—I was placated. Natural emotional expressions that fell outside of *happy* were met with impatience and often rage by my father. My mother responded with an anxious "you're okay" and a perfunctory hug and a pat on the back in a curt "there, there" fashion intended to soothe, but not coming close to matching my level of discomfort. (I happen to know this reassuring hug well, because as a nervous, young mother myself, I mindlessly repeated this pattern at times with my own child.) The cocktail of my dad's anger response paired with my mom's minimizing response knocked me unconscious to my own needs at an early age.

In my home, there were kisses goodnight, bandages on boo-boos, and healthy meals prepared from our abundant backyard garden. There were stylish clothes and constantly bleached Keds sneakers lined up in my closet. There were gifts aplenty under our sparkling Christmas tree, and there was even a rainbow painted on my bedroom wall. I had a Cocker Spaniel in the yard and a tabby cat curled up on my bed, a hula hoop and a trampoline and a Barbie beach house (where I would literally spend hours letting blonde Barbie and brunette Barbie make out, naked and clanking around on top of one another in their pink plastic Barbie bed, with Ken cast aside, face down in a pile of polyester dresses, and my heart racing at the idea of being caught by my parents).

The voices of those who dwelled inside my home during this formative time also dwell inside my head to this day. There was my perfectionistic, seething father, slamming the door when he got home from work and wiping his finger above each doorframe to search for dust and someone to blame it on if he found any. There were my mom's permanently clenched teeth, tight brow, and the deafening sound of her held breath. There were the bright blue eyes of my older sister, Kim, that she'd learned to hold wide open, and her abrupt, birdlike movements, performing everything expected of a firstborn in the most efficient and excellent way possible. My house smelled like Sunday morning chocolate chip pancakes and hypervigilance.

Recently, I had an oddly strong reaction to hearing my mom talk about the new Havanese puppy she adopted to keep her company during the COVID-19 pandemic. In the phone call describing her new dog, she said, "He's all personality! He puts on a show for everyone! He's not afraid of a thing. He's such a good boy—he's not even crying or whining. He doesn't even need to pee in the night. It's like he knows he has to hold back until we're awake." In my system, it viscerally felt like I was hearing the unveiled expectations my mom may have had of me as a child. Because my mom was innocently expressing love and admiration for her cute puppy, I was surprised that hearing this over the phone impacted me in such a tender place. I felt tears well up in my eyes, as though my body remembered that same vibe, coming from that same voice. Implicit in these benign remarks about a puppy was the idea passed down through generations of my family that we needed to hold back inconvenient needs for the sake of our caregivers. We came forward only when requested, to dazzle and to entertain. I unconsciously absorbed this as a child. Later, I consciously observed it in the rote expectations the grandparents nonchalantly placed upon our baby daughter. Newer beings are to acquiesce to the conventions of the elder beings who feed and shelter them. This is often the earliest experience we have of neglecting our own needs.

Even in writing this, there's a part of me anticipating the response that I'm drawing ridiculous conclusions—that I'm being too dramatic, too sensitive, or too serious. Sure, comparing a response to a puppy to my childhood is perhaps a nuanced bridge, but the spot it poked in my body's memory, in my emotional being, is unmistakably sore. Thankfully, that points me toward the personal growth work I still need to do, as my family members are simply being who they are.

Just as this pattern didn't begin with the puppy or the birth of my daughter, it also didn't begin with my own mom or my own childhood. Knowing my maternal grandparents and the culture in which they were steeped, I imagine my mom was raised in a very similar environment, as was her mom before her, and all the way up to the far-reaching branches of our family tree. I come from a long line of women who are givers. They give of themselves until they are empty. My maternal grandmother was known and praised for the way she cared for others over herself. These days, my mom makes custard for sick or dying friends and soups for the bereaved, which now happens often, given her age and her large social circle. Underneath the genuine love in her generous heart, I can sense her disappointment in that there's seemingly no one who can meet my mom with the sacrificial level of tending with which she meets others. Her selflessness was inherited, a learned survival technique to prioritize others' needs over

her own. Not to have the tantrum. Not to voice her preferences. I feel deep empathy for this piece of my mom
because it reminds me of the resentments and disappointments I have been working to release from my own
first half of life.

As women, we are taught that to speak our needs or
to ask for what we really want is selfish and a burden. It
would take up too much space. It would be impolite. We
learned how to be needed, not to need. We learned how
to be wanted, not to want. We learned how to be desired,
not to desire. The message in my family has always been
just to be a quiet, pretty, good girl and have faith that
others will love you for it, and a life will form around you
that you should be (you had better be!) so happy and
grateful to have.

POWER

In midlife, as I'm making some grown-ass-woman decisions, I bump up against another introject: I am not to
be trusted. I am not an expert. I am just a girl. I need
to consult authorities (or pretty much anyone outside
myself, especially males) to know if my decisions are valid.
Some fierce adult part inside me rages against this one, as
no one knows what it feels like to live in my body in this life.
Why would *they* know better than I do about living as *me*?

Giving power away to others is a damaging practice I
inherited—one that has taken diligent, conscious work in
my adult life thus far to dismantle. When I was a young
girl, I looked to my parents, teachers, and doctors to name
my experiences and to affirm my next steps. While these

authorities are usually well-meaning humans doing jobs they were trained to do, I was tragically disempowered.

I noticed it most when my daughter was a baby. I breastfed her every time she asked, which was every two hours, though it honestly felt like every five minutes because I lived topless on my couch under a Boppy pillow for almost fifteen months—in the era just before smart phones! I was freakin' present! Without reading the books on what to do with a new baby, Craig and I did all the things described in attachment parenting resources, though they were purely instinctual—birth bonding, breastfeeding, baby wearing, and co-sleeping. We tended to her every time she cried, and we never let her cry herself to sleep. Across the board, the older generations in our family didn't understand what we were doing. I wasn't breastfed as a child because it was the 1970s, and my mom's doctor told her that formula was better for babies than breast milk, and she trusted him (or rather, the baby formula sales rep who was wooing him) over trusting her own body, ready to spill forth this "useless" liquid gold. Anytime there was a difficulty in my new mommyhood life, like if my daughter's sleep patterns changed or she was fussy with teething, I would casually mention it to my mom. She would try to be supportive in saying, "Oh honey, I'm sorry. What did the doctor say?" It would confuse the hell out of me. Why would I call a doctor when a tooth was coming in or when there was a growth spurt? My mothering instincts knew what my daughter needed, but my own mother implied that my instincts were not to be trusted, as she has been taught not to trust her own. Intimidating women into depending on authorities over their own bodies is not unique to my family—it is certainly a systemic, cultural issue. It keeps our power in check.   ·

By the time I was a parent in my thirties, I had heard, "Well, what did the doctor/teacher/your boss say?" from my mom so many times that I figuratively stuck my fingers in my ears and shouted "la-la-la-la-la" every time her good-intentioned sentence began. I ran (perhaps too far) in the other direction, with a total "fuck authority!" attitude. I quit having jobs where I had a boss. I quit having doctors who were limited by capitalism and patriarchy. I became a psychotherapist, maybe in part so I could be a legitimate authority on my own emotional and spiritual well-being. Funny, though—even with my credentials, when I tell my mom about anything having to do with mental health, she just nods without acknowledging my statement and simply says, "All right, sweetie." Then she will read the very same thing years later somewhere on the internet, written by another "authority" (usually a male who has been on Oprah) and she'll say to me, "Did you know that so-and-so says . . .?" Clearly, I cannot be the authority. And she cannot be the authority, either. The repeated message is that we need to outsource our power to "the experts," many of whom are winging it, even as we lionize them.

LADIES

In the environment in which I came of age in the 1970s and '80s, biological sex and gender were absolutely conflated, and all humans were deemed heterosexual until proven otherwise. There were assumptions regarding clothes, toys, activities, romantic interests, and acceptable emotional expressions. As a baby, I was bald for a long time, but once I got my first wisp of blonde hair, my mom would lick her thumb and index finger, stick that one tuft of hair up straight, and slap a pink bow around it so people wouldn't mistake me for a boy. God forbid.

My mom talks about how when she was a kid, she was a "tomboy" —a common and now outdated phrase. Her childhood interest in things like climbing trees and playing sports were assigned as "boy" traits in generations before and including my own. Perhaps my mom's history of what she calls "playing as hard as the boys" gave me a bit of range as a girl who grew up in the rural farmland of Pungo in southern Virginia Beach. When I wasn't at school, I could wear my red Little Slugger baseball cap, cuffed jeans, flannels, and sneakers as my "play clothes," (or, it occurs to me as I write this, that perhaps it was me sporting some stereotypical baby-gay attire). My "school clothes" were mostly comprised of ironed dresses and shined shoes. I had matching ribbons for my hair, which was styled using uncomfortable pink sponge curlers that I wore overnight under a silk scarf my mom tied around my head.

Before I was born, my dad had wanted a boy he would have named Byron. When I was a child, I remember him telling me that he wanted to "toughen [me] up like a boy." He literally threw my skinny, tanned, six-year-old body off his boat in the middle of the Chesapeake Bay, without warning, as a first effort to teach me to swim. Kim, who was eight years older than me, dove in to save me from drowning. My dad called me a wimp when I cried about it. He nicknamed me Hemorrhoid for being "a pain in the ass." He repeatedly shamed me for wanting to spend time in the sanctuary of my bedroom, engrossed in imaginal play with my art supplies, stuffed animals, and typewriter. He forced me to go outside, which made the outdoors feel like punishment. He didn't allow me to get up from the dinner table until I had cleaned my plate, even though I disliked meat and fed it to the dog (or my sister) when no one was looking. He laughed audibly from the back deck when our rooster climbed onto my head and pecked my scalp until I bled. He didn't come to my aid. Afterward, as I sobbed about the whole incident, he said he wished I wasn't "such an overreacting drama queen." Thankfully, none of this served to toughen up my exquisite sensitivity, but it did cause me to shy away from taking risks, from relying on the strength of my body, from feeling comfortable in the ocean, from feeling safe outdoors, and from trusting my inner knowing around what I wanted to do or wear or eat.

I grew up with the idea that being "ladylike" was required, and that it was a virtue. If I didn't cross my legs properly or if I cursed or burped or farted, that was not ladylike. If I wore black sneakers or initiated a phone call to a boy, that wasn't ladylike. If I got angry or confrontational, that wasn't ladylike, either. All of these walls pushed in from different sides, telling me how I could and could not express myself in a female body, with a huge assumption that vulva owners wanted to express as "girls," and that girls naturally aimed to be "ladies." The ladies' room got very small and stuffy, very quickly.

I remember primping before a middle school dance one Friday evening before my mom came home from work. She was to drive me there as soon as she returned, so I put the finishing touches on my supercool, preteen look—a blue and white Benetton sweatshirt, matching blue stirrup pants, white Keds, blue eyeshadow, rosy blush, and some pink iridescent lip gloss. Hello, 1987! I'll never forget my mom coming in the door and immediately wiping both her hands across my pink cheeks, exclaiming "You look like a hussy!" because she disapproved of my heavy, novice blush application. In that moment, I wondered what it meant to be a "hussy." Did that mean I was too ladylike? Was I too much of a sexual being? The ladies' room walls closed in tighter.

When I was in eighth grade, I was *obsessed* with the glam rock band Poison. I covered every inch of my bedroom walls with their life-sized posters and flashy centerfolds I tore from *Metal Edge* magazine. The four men in the band all had long hair, teased to '80s perfection, and they wore so much makeup that my mom would have called them hussies, too. I was smitten with Bret Michaels, the lead singer. I thought he was the prettiest man in the universe. My mom came into my room one evening and as we were talking, I commented to her about how good-looking I thought the band members were. She turned to inspect the posters of these men in all their androgynous, glittered glory and said, "Jen! They look just like women! Are you a lesbian or something?" At that time, I would not have said that I was, but my stomach certainly flipped.

SEX

I think about sex whenever I see the painting *I and the Village*, by Marc Chagall. Yeah, that's weird. Let me explain. From second through sixth grades, I attended a Gifted and Talented program one day a week at another school in my city. My family called it "Gifted" for short, which eventually became a sarcastic nickname for me whenever I did something foolish or got something wrong as a child. They were teasing me, but I suppose it was an upgrade over my dad calling me Hemorrhoid.

In second grade, on my very first day of Gifted, I remember sitting alone, eating lunch in this new, unfamiliar cafeteria. I was staring at a large replica of that Chagall painting beside my lunch table while eavesdropping on the conversation of some nearby sixth graders. They were talking about how "humping" means that "the man puts his penis into the woman's vagina." And there was wide-eyed, seven-year-old me, eating my peanut butter and jelly sandwich out of my Muppets lunchbox, intently focused on a painting of a green-faced man and a cow looking into each other's eyes.

That evening, while my mom stirred her homemade marinara sauce on the stove, I looked up at her and said, "I know what humping is," and I proceeded to recite the sentence I had heard in the lunchroom about penises and vaginas. I'll never forget the stunned look on her face when she looked down at me and just said, "Go tell your dad." Of course, I did not go tell my dad, as he was super intimidating and the last person on Earth I wanted to talk with about sex. Instead, I went to my room and told my diary.

When I was ten, I rode to Lynnhaven Mall in the passenger seat of my mom's gray Honda Prelude, her post-divorce wheels. She was chewing Wrigley's Doublemint gum, happily humming, and tapping her Revlon Rosewine–painted fingernails on the steering wheel to the beat of Madonna's "Like a Virgin" playing on the radio. I watched the raindrops splay across the glass of the passenger window as we picked up speed. I listened to the lyrics, trying to understand, and I finally worked up the courage to ask out loud, "Mom, what's a virgin?" Her humming and tapping stopped. She was silent for a moment and then said, "It's just someone with very little experience." I didn't ask anything else, she didn't say anything more, and eventually she began to hum again, in a loud, strained way.

As a child, I was told that sex was only to be shared between a husband and a wife, purely for procreation. My parents' discomfort around these discussions suggested that sex was too private to talk about. There is a story in my family that my mom's mom, whom I called Nana, was so modest about sex that my grandfather never once saw her naked in their 49 years of marriage—that she would always undress in her closet and emerge only once the lights were off. Whether or not that story was entirely true, it is what we kids were meant to believe. We never had the "birds and bees" talk in my house. Nor did my parents sign the permission slip allowing me to take sex education at school. Of course, sex ed was absolutely worthless in the '80s, advocating abstinence and promoting the damaging, antiquated social construct of virginity, so perhaps it was for the better that I didn't attend. When it came to sex, there was a shroud of secrecy, a fear of being stigmatized, and deep-rooted shame.

PUBERTY

Throughout grade school, I had a short bookshelf against the back wall of my closet, under the hanging clothes. All my books were there, except for a collection from Kim. The books she handed down to me were kept on a shelf way up high, near the closet ceiling. I would stand on my bed, tilt my head to the right, and squint to read their spines: *Are You There, God? It's Me, Margaret*; *Deenie*; *Then Again, Maybe I Won't*; *Tiger Eyes*—a whole Judy Blume collection. Most girls who came of age in the 1980s know that these books were that era's holy grail of pubescent wisdom.

My mom and sister both told me I wasn't old enough to read these books. When I asked why, my sister said, "Because they're about getting your period." I asked what a period was, and my mom said, "It's punctuation at the end of a sentence."

More than feeling highly suspicious of this explanation, I felt left out. I felt that a lot as the youngest child. My mom and Kim are only eighteen years apart, and they often get mistaken for sisters, especially because they have similar mannerisms, styles, and social circles. To me, they have always felt like best friends rather than mother and daughter.

One of our "funny" family stories is that one night when I was about six years old and Kim was fourteen, I burst into audible sobs while in the bathtub. My mom heard me crying from down the hall and came in, wondering what happened. I wailed, "When I'm Kim's age, you're going to be an old lady!" Part of me wanted to grow up faster and catch up so I could fit in, be included, and be their BFF, too. I would finally be in on the hushed conversations that stopped the moment I entered a room. I would have my period and a bra and makeup. I would have a boyfriend and follow the family tradition of being a cheerleader.

When I was about ten years old, after I wore her down by repeatedly asking about menstruation, my mom brought me into her bedroom, grabbed the yellow legal pad we used for our weekly grocery list, and drew a diagram of what looked like the skull of a farm animal. She told me about ovaries and fallopian tubes and eggs, as if she had studied the female reproductive system in our dusty set of World Book encyclopedias while cooking dinner. I nodded along, and maybe two minutes later, the first and only menstruation and sex talk we'd ever had was over.

A couple years later, on a Saturday morning in October, while sitting on the toilet in the bathroom attached to my bedroom, I saw the much-welcomed sight of blood in my underwear. To say it was welcomed is an understatement because, like Margaret in Judy Blume's book, I had been praying for this moment for nearly four years, writing about this longing almost nightly in my journals. I was the youngest kid in my grade, thus the last one among my friends to start menstruating. I cried tears of joy when I saw the stain in my underwear that day.

I called out to my mom to come into my bathroom. I expected her to show me how to wear a pad and a tampon. I was also partially expecting her to be sappy and cry and say, "My baby is growing up!" I did not expect her to throw me a celebratory dinner party or to create a red tent or moon-lodge ceremony (that's not how she rolls), but being the witch I already was, I did secretly dream about that sort of ritual welcoming me into womanhood.

None of those exact scenarios manifested, but my mom did show up in my bathroom that morning. Without much fanfare, she handed me a package of the bulkiest pads you can imagine. I fumbled to remove the adhesive backing and glue one to my underwear. A few hours later,

I had to put on my cheerleading uniform, which included thick, tight, dark-green bloomers. Bloomers are basically uniform-colored underwear covers that go under one's cheerleading skirt. In my inherited shame around being in a bleeding, female body, I was horrified to think that I would have to cartwheel across the football field in a matter of hours with my cheerleading squad. I feared they would all see the giant bulky, pad in my underwear.

A couple months into this nonsense, I asked my mom if I could use tampons instead of those enormous pads. She said I wasn't allowed to wear tampons because my grandmother (her mom, my Nana) would be angry; Nana thought that only girls who were not virgins could use tampons. I was told that if Nana ever saw tampons in my bathroom, my mom and I would both be in trouble. So, I wore the maxiest of pads for nearly a year because my mom subscribed to her mom's ignorance. Eventually, I rebelled and bought my own tampons with my allowance when I was at a grocery store with a friend. I told my mom I would hide them if Nana visited. It was bizarre to feel shame about inserting cotton into my vagina. That shame was compounded with the deeper shame that would someday be upon me when I became sexually active. This was my rite of passage into puberty. This is my blueprint.

ENOUGH

My parents were high-school sweethearts—the cheer-leader and the bad boy. Every time I look at the photograph my grandfather took of the two of them in my grandparents' pristine, don't-touch-anything living room in 1967, as they were gorgeously dressed for their senior prom, I remember how my parents were on the brink of pregnancy and would elope only a few months after that picture was taken.

They stayed married for seventeen years, until one June evening when my dad confessed to my mom that he had been having an affair with Phyllis from work and that he would be moving out. The night that happened, I had a friend visiting for a sleepover, and we were playing on the swing set in the backyard when my mom came out to tell my friend she had to go home because we were having "a family emergency." After my friend got picked up, I went to my room and played records while I anxiously awaited hearing about the emergency. My dad came in and told my little nine-year-old self that he was going on a business trip. Then he packed up his red Toyota pickup truck and left. I knew a work trip could not be the family emergency, but I didn't ask questions.

Understandably, my mom was devastated. She cried for about two years straight. Every time I walked past her bedroom door and saw the curtains drawn and her crying on her bed, I cried, too. I recall my dad stopping by once to retrieve more of his things, and I snuck out to the driveway to put a Fishy Phyllis Garbage Pail Kid sticker on the bumper of his truck. I remember calling her Syphilis instead of Phyllis, something I didn't understand at age nine, but had heard my mom say when talking on the phone to her friends.

One evening after dinner, my mom put me into the Prelude, and we drove for about half an hour to a busy street I had never seen before. Mom parallel-parked strategically so our car windows aligned with an alley. "Do you see your dad's truck parked down there?" she asked me, as I had a better view down the alley from the passenger seat of the car. What was more dangerous than the fact that I was riding in the front seat of the car at nine years old (hey, it was the '80s) was that I was helping my (literally and figuratively) green-eyed mother stalk my father at his mistress's apartment. I saw his red truck. "Yes . . . ?" I meekly replied to her question. Now she saw red and pounded the steering wheel, with restraint and only once. Her chin quivered as she held back tears on the drive home.

Under her sadness, I sensed that my mom felt shame about my dad leaving for another woman, as if it had been her duty to keep him. As if she'd failed after trying so hard. I remember feeling ashamed, as well, that my dad wanted a divorce, because it felt as though he wanted to divorce us all. I grew up carrying the feeling that I was not enough. I hid my parents' separation from my friends for almost two years, not inviting anyone over to my house and lying about where my dad was when asked. Even though my mom tried her best to help us see our dad after he moved out, he did virtually nothing to maintain a relationship with me and Kim. I saw him a couple times a year for the next decade, but only when my mom or Kim would initiate a visit for us. We were completely estranged by the time I was eighteen. That year, he declined the invitation to Kim's wedding, saying he felt too ashamed to show his face among our family and friends. For the first time in my life, I stood up to my dad, challenging him to set his own feelings aside for the sake of my sister on her wedding day. I also told him that after years of our pursuing him, he'd have to be the one to reach out the next time we talked. All contact between us ceased after that phone call.

The combination of my dad's indiscretions and my mom's reaction to the situation created my prototype for romantic love. When it came to relationships (all of them being between a man and a woman in the framework of my family and our social circles), the message I received was that the woman needed to be enough (pretty enough, agreeable enough, helpful enough, quiet enough, sexy enough, talented enough, a good-enough cook/house-keeper/mother) to keep her man from straying. I watched my mom sacrifice the discovery of her passions to be a housewife and full-time mother. She was the wife who freshly ironed all her husband's clothes, cooked all the meals, and cleaned up afterwards. She kept herself well-groomed and in shape, with gorgeous hair and perfect clothes. At a very early age, even though it may not have been said out loud, I absorbed the message that if your husband's attention (even a glance) was directed toward another woman, shame on *you*. That's right, shame on the woman who could not keep her man happy and engaged. I learned that the male gaze is something to be won. Jealousy is a toxin that runs through my blood. It is not entirely mine, but it has caused every level of fresh hell in my relationships. It planted an ugly seed in the loam of my formative years, and it grew into the most poisonous ivy, winding its vines tightly around my heart. My dad's depar-ture without any explanation when I was nine, coupled with his cutting off contact completely when I was eigh-teen, left abandonment wounds I work daily to heal, so as not to act through them.

I deeply long to feel special and to be chosen. However, in past romantic relationships, I unreasonably wanted to be the *only* person my partner found attractive. Otherwise, as the messaging suggested, I would be abandoned. My first long-term relationship with Jim, from thirteen through eighteen, ended after Jim confessed to several instances of cheating on me with other girls. After Jim, I spent nearly four years with a 6'7" guy who fronted an indie-emo-punk-rock band and garnered all sorts of attention for his height and talent. Naturally, I was intensely insecure in that relationship, losing my true self while trying to become someone I thought he wouldn't leave. Ultimately, he didn't cheat or leave, but I got sick of the fangirl I had become with him. That breakup at twenty-two years old was my last major one before meeting Craig. The end of the relationship with the rockstar was the impetus for seeking my first therapist, for seeking myself, for seeking the truth of my sexuality, for seeking my wildness, for seeking to unwind all these maladaptive forms of domestication.

ATTACHMENT

At a very young age, our primary caregivers are our only representation of the larger world. Our nervous systems are designed to scan our early experiences for threats to our safety. If we cry and our needs are not met, we may feel abandoned. If we are not nourished by touch or eye contact, we may feel unloved. Our systems are brilliant at forming adaptive strategies around these sorts of experiences. The adjustments we make to maintain

.

connection become the way we attach or relate to others as adults.

According to John Bowlby and Mary Ainsworth's modern attachment theory,[2] there are four main styles of attachment that are formed in the bond we have with our first caregivers. These styles can even begin when we are in the womb, and they affect how we are in our relationships throughout our lives. I'll give a very simple flavor of the styles here for our purposes. The first style is securely attached, wherein a child experiences their parent as a secure base and, thus, can feel confident, connected, and trusting in their relationships later in life. Another type is dismissive-avoidant, which describes those who are emotionally independent and are uncomfortable getting too close to others, often as a result of an absent or neglectful caregiver. A third attachment style is anxious-preoccupied, which is the category of people who crave intimacy and need a lot of responsiveness and reassurance from their partners, generally due to inconsistent parenting, emotionally unavailable caregivers, and/or an experience of abandonment. The final style is known as disorganized or fearful-avoidant, which essentially looks like alternating dismissive-avoidant and anxious-preoccupied styles in that the person craves closeness but when they get it, they push it away. This style is often the result of childhood trauma, living in a household of addiction or abuse, or one where active harm is coming from the person who is supposed to be taking care of the child.

---

2   From John Bowlby, *A Secure Base* (New York: Basic Books, 1988).

In psychology speak, I have an anxious-preoccupied attachment style, as does most of the population. Good-byes shatter me. I can feel abandoned in a casual parting or when my invitations are declined. I have terrible FOMO when my friends plan something I cannot attend. It is easy for me to fall into the timeworn groove of feeling left out or lonely when relationships feel inconsistent.

I have a memory of being a little girl, maybe seven-years-old, hiding in the nook of my favorite tree in the woods behind my house when my dad made me go outside. I'd bring sugar cubes and carrots to feed to the neighbor's horses, just over the fence in which my tree was entangled. To most kids, this was called "playing out-side." I clearly remember pretending I was having fun, as if someone was watching and judging my level of enjoyment, thinking to themself, "Yep, just a little girl frolicking happily in the woods. I'm comfortable with that." (Introject: Don't ever make adults feel uncomfortable.) I'd listen to sticks and twigs mysteriously breaking around me, watch leaves sail downward in zigzagged paths, become entranced by the way the wind shifted the dappled sunlight on tree trunks. I'd look at the leaf decay on the ground, random car parts, and bits of trash here and there. Fear would be ever-present in my body while I pretended to play in the woods, yet the more prominent emotion was loneliness.

I once told an EMDR therapist about this memory, and she immediately asked if I knew whether I was a twin in utero. To my knowledge, I was not. Her question had made me sob, as I had always felt the void of a female compan-ion—like I was alone but should not be. I had sought to fill this emptiness. I looked for her in friendships, both in passed notes in grade school and pieces of text messages as an adult, analyzing the fold of the note or the use of emojis to determine if I was welcomed, accepted, loved. I replayed conversations. I scanned eyes. I watched the way hands would reach toward me, or the way they would not. The way my phone would ring, or the way it would not. I grieved the loss of a connection I had not yet had.

At a preverbal stage, we learn that to have our needs met and to be consistently cared for, we are not to disturb the homeostasis of our caregivers or our home, which often means suppressing the fullest expression of our authenticity. In this way, we subtly and slowly become domesticated. We are cut off from our wildness, our human animal impulses. We begin to value who we think we *should be* over who we *are*. Through years of conditioning and habit, this survival mechanism can become an identity. As human beings, we are brilliant at how to keep ourselves alive and safe, adaptable to many environments and resilient to much adversity.

In midlife, as we individuate from familial and societal messaging, it is a prime time to look back over the introjects we received from these influential groups. We now have the ability to make conscious what we unconsciously accepted at a young age. As adults, we no longer need to buy into these notions in order to survive.

WRITE

It's time to explore some of the introjects, messaging, conditioning, indoctrination, and rules you carry from your lineage, family, environment, and culture. Grab your journal and write each of the prompts below at the top of its own page. Set a timer and spend one minute with each one, listing anything and everything that comes to mind.

Note that I have written "primary caregiver" as the figure to whom you first formed an attachment. Feel free to change this to the name of whomever this was for you. It could be "Mom" and/or "Dad" or "parents" or "grandparents," etc. You may even find it powerful to make a separate list for each caregiver in each category as the messages we receive from different people often vary and even conflict.

- What I learned from my primary caregiver about my needs was . . .

- What I learned from my culture/ society about my needs was . . .

- What I learned from my primary caregiver about power was . . .

- What I learned from my culture/ society about power was . . .

- What I learned from my primary caregiver about intimacy was . . .

- What I learned from my culture/ society about intimacy was . . .

- What I learned from my primary caregiver about self-expression was . . .

- What I learned from my culture/ society about self-expression was . . .

- What I learned from my primary caregiver about spirituality was . . .

- What I learned from my culture/ society about spirituality was . . .

CREATE

For this activity, you'll need any preferred art materials and a piece of paper. You'll use these to create a family constellation drawing.

Make a symbol representing each family member and/or caregiver who resided in your household and was a direct influence on you as a child. Include yourself in the drawing. You may wish to organize the symbols as a family tree or by degrees of closeness to you. Draw a line or arrow from the symbol of each person to the symbol that represents you. Allow the shape, color, and pressure you use for each line to indicate, in your own visual language, how you feel about that relationship. One may be loopy and aqua and another jagged and black. Write words or feelings along the line that indicate the message and/or energy you received from that person. It is often helpful to have these relationships externalized on the page, allowing you to perceive them from a safe distance outside of yourself as you begin to uncover your childhood introjects.

ALTAR RITUAL

Find a photograph of yourself as a baby or child and place this image on your midlife emergence altar. Keep this photograph on your altar as a reminder of the authenticity of the self—the soul—you came into this life to be. You may even wish to put another childhood photo on your bathroom mirror or the dashboard of your car. Look at the photograph(s) of your younger self with compassion, empathy, and love for taking in all the messages and rules you needed to survive. Thank this little one for keeping you safe, for getting you to where you are today. If you don't have any childhood photographs available, draw, write, or create something that resonates with you to represent your younger self, and use it in place of the photograph mentioned above.

CHAPTER 4

becoming
visible

*The human soul doesn't want to be advised or fixed
or saved. It simply wants to be witnessed—to be
seen, heard, and companioned exactly as it is.*

PARKER PALMER *MY MISGIVINGS ABOUT ADVICE*

INVITATION

In reflecting upon my childhood, it became clear to me that a key part of how I stayed safe and assured my belonging and acceptance was to stifle anything in me that felt like "too much": my needs, my power, my intuition, my fears, my anger. I repressed the many ways in which I felt unconventional, including, but certainly not limited to, my desires around intimacy and sex. The invisibility of this piece, particularly my queerness, had been so ceaseless that it felt white hot, searing a hole in my heart with every passing day it went unseen. After Craig and I began to explore the idea of having an open relationship, acting upon my innermost truths was building an enticing momentum.

The next healing step for me was to allow previously camouflaged aspects of myself to become more visible, beyond just sharing them with Craig. I had confessions brewing inside me around three things that felt absolutely edgy to expose: my desire to explore intimacy with women, the fact that Craig and I had opened up our marriage, and the fact that I found myself attracted to my married, female best friend.

While contemplating how to make these painfully unseen pieces of me seen, I felt the vulnerability one might feel when "coming out of the closet." However, this term feels vehemently incorrect to me, as it panders to assumptions of heteronormativity. By saying "coming out," we continue to accentuate queerness as "other," rather than normalizing it. The idea of "coming out" places the responsibility on the queer person to correct wrongful assumptions about sexual or gender identity. Many people in the LGBTQ+ community, myself included, prefer terms like *letting in* or *inviting in* over *coming out*. Words are spells; they carry energy, and they matter deeply. It feels more self-loving and in alignment for me to say that, by becoming visible, I'm inviting others to get to know me. It was absolutely time to reveal more of myself to my loved ones.

I certainly didn't have a grand "coming out" moment around my sexuality in childhood, and I didn't broach the subject very formally in my early twenties. I imagine there may not have been validation or acceptance at the time, but at the very least, I needed the recognition and acknowledgement. Since my forty-first birthday, I had been throwing the most precious and tender pieces of my heart into the air, not knowing where they would land. It was time for me to have an "inviting in" of sorts.

ELECTRIC

Throughout 2017, the year I was in the workshop along-side Emily, she had been privy to daily updates on the evolution of my emerging sexuality and the changes in my marriage. She and Craig were my sole confidants. The next action I knew I needed to take was to tell Emily directly about my feelings for her. Our friendship was perhaps at its closest iteration during that summer. I was traveling to Boulder monthly and staying with her for the workshop in which we were participants. We would wake up together groggily, process our nighttime dreams over tea and coffee, put on mascara and the essential oil blend we both wear, and help each other decide which talismans would be both fashionable and meaningful to wear for the day. We would drive from her Denver home to the spot just up the mountain from Boulder and sing along to our collaborative playlist. We would share our personal growth in our workshop circle of twenty. Then we would come home together and have even deeper talks in our closed circle of two while cooking dinner, sharing cocktails, and lying on a blanket in her backyard looking at the stars. We would say our goodnights and retire to separate bedrooms.

In July 2017, when I visited for the second weekend of our women's circle, there were other guests in her home, so I rented an Airbnb on the main drag in downtown

Boulder. After an intense day of the workshop, Emily came back to my tiny, rented cottage and decided she would stay the night with me. We opened a bottle of wine and discussed the day's events. Once we were buzzed and hungry, we stumbled through warm drizzle to an eclectic downtown restaurant for dinner.

We were seated in a corner booth in the dark, cozy basement of the place. As our server brought a bottle of red wine to our table, we both noticed that the conversation felt heavy with the weight of something unsaid. "What is it?" Emily gently asked, tilting her head and softening her oceanic eyes. I felt the magma of truth squeeze up through the fissures the wine had opened in my thinning inner walls. I desperately wanted to be the most magnetic, sexy, confident version of myself in that moment—the wild, wise, witchy creatrix. The irresistible one we all want to muster when professing our love to another. *And I so was not.* I immediately became a drunken, sobbing, snotty mess. My voice squeaked and quivered. Often when we are being our bravest, we feel the most disempowered, vulnerable, and small. Even though I felt shame for having these parts of myself come forward, I also wanted these messy parts to be adored.

Confessions toppled drunkenly and ceaselessly from my lips, across the untouched food and the votive candle and the empty glasses of wine, and into her ears. In the rare moments when I wasn't blotting tears and snot from my face, she reached her hands across the table and held both my hands in hers.

First, I told her about an evening, twelve years prior, when I was driving home from the mall, having spent the whole day with her shopping for dresses to wear to our graduation from Naropa. At the time, I was six years into my relationship with Craig (two years into our marriage), and she was almost eleven years into a committed relationship with the boyfriend she had met as an undergraduate. On the stretch of highway between the mall and my apartment, I felt a fluttering in my stomach thinking about my undeniable attraction to her and how gratifying our shared intimacy felt. I fantasized about confessing these thoughts about Emily to Craig once I got home and considered how they might free us to live a different life.

I often thought of that late '90s Gwyneth Paltrow movie, *Sliding Doors*, where the viewers get to see how the main character's life unfolds in two parallel story lines. In one plot, her character catches a train in time to find her boyfriend cheating, empowering her into a major glow up in all areas of her life. In the alternate scenario, she misses that same train, thus living a meek and unaware existence, simply due to the seemingly insignificant variable of which train she took home.

I told Emily about the gusty night we spent glamping (I don't camp) along the Pacific coast when she had visited me in California a year ago, and how, despite the fact that our glampsite came equipped with comfortable beds and heated blankets, I couldn't sleep a wink. My feelings for her were demandingly banging on the inner chambers of my heart even more mightily than the wild wind banged on the canvas walls of that metal-framed bungalow.

I revealed what had been in my heart on an evening in Sonoma just a month earlier, when we were sitting on the balcony of our Airbnb, tipsy from a day of winery tours. I told her how badly I wanted to kiss her when we left to go on a stargazing walk. About how that was the reason I had suddenly fallen silent that night after all the shared giggles.

I confessed that I had been attracted to her for years and that our recent emotional and spiritual intimacy had heightened to a fever pitch I could no longer ignore. I wondered out loud, to her and to myself, if what I really wanted was to express love more through my previously bound and braced body, as I had held myself to such strict standards regarding physical touch outside of my marriage. I began to question the binary of friendship versus romance. The line between those now felt like one I did not invent and could not comprehend. I was working on a way to reconcile my hunger for deeper intimacy in a culture where this dichotomy is so unnaturally pronounced. I spoke of how I feared my confession could damage our friendship. I reiterated that I had such profound respect for her marriage. And regrettably, I still could not contain these feelings, even though I had tried.

I could sense her stupefaction and anxiety as she graciously listened and cried with me. She told me how flattered she was and how much she loved me. She assured me that she would stay right there, as my friend, and that we would get through this.

The server brought a to-go box for the dinner I hadn't touched, and Emily and I found ourselves back on the rainy sidewalk in downtown Boulder, walking and crying, arms linked. She plucked a mugwort cigarette from her bag, and we paused under the eaves of the downtown's only bodega to take shelter from the rain. I pulled the hood of my giant black raincoat over my head and leaned against the concrete wall. Both of us took turns pulling drags from this dream-inducing, herbal joint. Suddenly, I felt ablaze, like a rebellious, invincible adolescent. Even though the talk had been difficult, I tasted what seemed like an entrancing cocktail of freedom and possibility— perhaps a high merely from the act of the invisible being made visible, and the healing in having it received with such gentleness. We walked back to the Airbnb, where we put on pajamas and climbed into the tiny double bed together. While Emily seemed to be sleeping soundly, my attempts to sleep that night were futile as I could viscerally feel the electricity in the stormy night air.

COVEN

Through the fall and winter that followed, while living states apart, Emily and I stayed in constant contact with one another, texting every day, sharing songs on our playl-ist, and talking on the phone a couple times a week. Emily and I are part of a group of friends from graduate school with whom we stayed close for the years after. Five of us comprise what I like to call our coven, because, well, we're witches—healing arts practitioners, magic makers, cre-ators. I was the only one of the five not living in Colorado at the time, so we held monthly council sessions via video conferencing where we shared deeply from our hearts. Despite the candor of our sharing, Emily and I hadn't told any of our friends about my emerging feelings.

In February 2018, my family traveled to Colorado to put an offer on the house we later ended up buying. During this trip, I was sick with a major cold that rendered me completely voiceless. There was that auspicious laryngitis, popping up once again at a vital moment. While visiting, the coven decided to hold council in person. It was hard enough to conceal in our virtual gatherings, but I knew I could not sit in a room with the women I loved so dearly and not speak about the undercurrent—the flow of my heart toward Emily. I talked with Emily privately beforehand about my hope to reveal this in our coven's council, and she said she would support me however I needed.

It was with trembling hands that I picked up the talking piece first that afternoon. With Emily's wife in the adjacent room, I was beyond uneasy and ungrounded but determined to peel back another layer in this space, because I knew it was safe enough. Through laryngitis and deep sobs, I whispered my secret to our shared coven of best friends. While it was terrifying to speak, it was also healing to hear my quiet, loud truth linger in the air of that room, to watch the faces of my friends as they heard me and held me in it. Each woman showed her own flavor of support and curiosity. Sharing on that day served to open the door to my self-imposed cage a bit wider. In the acknowledgement I received, I didn't gain peace or satisfaction, but I could taste a freedom I had never felt before.

SEEN

Even though I constantly teeter between the desire to be seen and the desire to hide, my aim is to engage in vulnerable self-expression whenever it feels available. Nothing piques my interest and arouses my curiosity more than to access and bare my rawness, and to see, hear, and feel others doing the same. This is a doorway to intimacy, to connection, to community, which is something we deeply crave as human beings. It's how we are wired.

I used to stew in my discomfort and disappointment of residing in the middle ground between the longing and the fear of being seen. In times when I've felt invisible, I've wondered, "Why aren't the people I love able to see and reflect me?" It occurred to me that this was an issue of perspective. Instead of feeling desperately unseen, I shifted my lens to recognize that the onus was on me to *make myself visible*. This was a more empowered stance, as it was one I could control. I had to bear the awkwardness of learning transparent yet well-boundaried, authentic self-expression.

Why is visibility so important? From my own experience, I can say that the process of expressing myself, being witnessed in that expression, and being reflected helps me to see and know myself more clearly and completely. In my trusted circles, I often share from an emergent edge; thus, what I am revealing is fresh. I am creating who I am becoming, as the words or images form in midair and are validated. This feels risky because it is the opposite of having everything together before presenting it—it is akin to the artist showing their process or the mathematician demonstrating their work. Letting our unformed, emergent edges be seen defies the mainstream, masculine culture's way of waiting until the thing we have made or the person we've become is polished and presentable. When we share ourselves, especially a piece that is new, there's a temptation to rehearse and have all our shit together first. That was the way I operated until my midlife emergence, when I began to discover the rewards of becoming visible in the unfolding moment, in a container of safety. I wanted to stand for and model the idea that formlessness is welcome, experimentation is encouraged, shapeshifting is natural, and sharing our unpolished humanness not only makes us more accessible, but it's also alluring. This way of life thwarts the patriarchy.

Patriarchy is a term used to describe the social system of gender-based hierarchy that assigns the most power to men and higher value to maleness, and "masculine" traits. In Western culture, masculine traits have been mostly linear, cerebral, logical, assertive, and unemotional. Feminine traits have generally been nonlinear, compassionate, wild, receptive, and emotional. Patriarchy perpetuates polarity, duality, separation, and oppression of women and gender-nonconforming people. In the world we're living in, revealing our unformed truths feels like a radical act. The paradigm that's emerging in our culture suggests that the way we show up can no longer be dictated by the linear, top-down shoulds that the patriarchy imposes— rather, this new movement is guided by pushing the edge of the wild, feminine mystery.

My inner critic, who has been conditioned as a good girl following the patriarchy, gets activated around my need to be witnessed. This judgmental voice asks if my need to be seen is driven by vanity, self-importance, insecurity, or early attachment wounds. Expression for its own sake is a worthy pursuit, as our thoughts and emotions need to move through and out of us in order for us to remain healthy, so that we don't languish until we rot or fester until we explode. However, being seen by another completes the loop because of the connection it invites. As our expressions are digested by someone else, we will receive their emotions, their stories, their thoughts. Understanding the impact our truths have on others can be heart-opening and beautiful, and it can also mean we grapple with rejections and projections.

Visibility is tricky because, like most things that can cause us to shed inhibitions, it often comes with hangovers. As living beings, after we experience any sort of expansion, we naturally experience a contraction—this cycle is as natural as breath, tides, moon cycles, seasons. For me, there are two flavors of contraction that I call visibility hangovers: the overshare hangover and the undershare hangover. When we put ourselves out there, perhaps in a new context or one that stretches us a little bit beyond our comfort zone, afterwards we tend to tighten into what I call an overshare hangover. Overshare hangovers feel like, "Oh shit, I said [or did or was] too much!" Then comes the urge to apply the weighted blanket in bed + purring cat + dark chocolate. The flip side might feel more subtle to many of us, especially if we live it so consistently that we just see it as the color of life: the undershare hangover, when we're not allowing parts of ourselves to be visible that long to be seen. You may be able to taste it when trying to connect with someone, then you come away from the situation should-ing on yourself. Like, "Fuck, I didn't even show who I am! I should have said . . ." In other words, it's the feeling of "I'm not enough." This is the deep longing we all have to be seen and heard in our fullness. Between these two, I personally feel like Goldilocks—trying to get my self-expression just right, or at least in a place where I feel congruent and satisfied, both appropriately enigmatic and adequately revealed.

Slowly opening to my loved ones, in safe circles, about my sexuality and endeavors in polyamory was both wildly exhilarating and absolutely terrifying to a recovering people-pleaser. However, I must follow the calling that it is part of my midlife mission to allow my internal grist to be a platform for lighting the way toward this sort of emergence. Writer Jeanette LeBlanc says, "To be human is to have needs. To speak them is wild reclamation. To be met inside of them is a holy miracle."

WRITE

This exercise is one of my favorite writing prompts for being seen in your full expression, without needing to be polite. You can do this journaling prompt in a list format, using your own memories or current experiences as material.

Begin each sentence with the statement: *"When I said ___, I really meant ___."*

Write as many of these statements as you wish. It's a way to get right with your soul on how you express exactly what you want to say and how you would like to say it. Strip it of the sugar coating, the niceties, the "good girl" conditioning. Just write your truth in each statement. Don't be surprised if each one becomes its own paragraph, page, or short story to flesh out later. This is a powerful way to retrain our brains and carve new neuropathways around how we can own and tell our truths using our most authentic voices.

More questions for written contemplation:

- Is your midlife longing already expressed in any part of your life? Where? Who in your life feels safe enough to hold your truths?

- Of those to whom you've not yet revealed your full self, with whom do you desire

103

to make these pieces of you visible?
What might that visibility elicit?

- Who are you terrified to have see
these pieces of you? What do you
fear about that happening?

- What type of support do you need to
bare yourself, stripped down to just
your simple truths, and shine visibly?
What support do you already have?

CREATE

Trace a circle in the center of a blank page. Collage
or draw images and/or write words inside the circle
to show what you are keeping hidden on the inside.
Use the space outside the circle to represent what
you reveal to others. Tip: You can trace a mug,
plate, or bowl—whichever fills the size of your
page best. When you are finished, look over your
image and decide whether the level of congruence
between internal and external is satisfactory.

ALTAR RITUAL

Find an object that represents whatever feelings
arise in you when you think about or write
about visibility. It could be a stone, a seashell,
a photograph, a doodle, a paper with a poem
or word on it, a piece of jewelry, or any sort of

talisman that holds the energy of being absolutely and utterly seen. Place it upon your midlife emergence altar. Whenever you see it there, let it see you.

CHAPTER 5

reclaiming the wild

Being tame is what we're taught: . . .
Put the crayons back, stay in line, don't talk too loud,
keep your knees together, nice girls don't . . .
As you might know, nice girls DO, and they like to
feel wild and alive. Being tame feels safe, being
wild, unsafe. Yet safety is an illusion anyway. We are
not in control . . . Living wild is its own reward.

SARK *SUCCULENT WILD WOMAN*

FIREFLIES

As a child, I was fascinated by fireflies. In Virginia, we called them lightning bugs. I would go outside after dinner in the summer and watch the fireflies hover around the flower-beds of azaleas and impatiens. Sometimes I captured a few in a Ball jar, secured plastic wrap on top with a rubber band, and poked lots of air holes in it. I used it as a night-light in my bedroom and let them go in the morning.

As a vegetarian with some Buddhist sensibilities, I hate to admit this, but I also remember pulling the glowing abdomens off the fireflies and spreading their biolumi-nescent matter across my face like war paint. I would run around my yard with a large hiking stick I had whittled on our only family camping trip ever, pretending (or perhaps knowing) that I was a fire warrior. I would yell chants and songs to let out the wildness that was not okay for me to express when I was sitting with my neatly folded napkin on my lap at the dinner table.

In my mid-twenties, I went to see an energy worker who told me that my inner child was holding my fire ele-ment captive—that I had left behind that part of myself when moving into adulthood. In that session, I envisioned myself as that small, glow-painted child holding a giant torch and setting fire to the forest behind my house as an act of freedom and cleansing. Afterwards, I went home and painted the fire girl on a huge canvas.

I brought the painting to one of my art therapy profes-sors when we were studying inner child work, and I felt like she saw and understood my fiery parts. A couple years later, when I graduated from that program, this beloved teacher created a piece of art for me upon which she wrote, "Remember your fire . . . Remember your fire . . . Remember your fire . . ." around its perimeter. This hangs in my art studio cabinet to this day.

I've hauled my fire girl painting from home to home over the years, usually keeping it in my basement or garage. I've worked extensively with this image, remem-bering my wildfire, spark by spark. When I hit midlife, I felt that fire burning so hot that I could not put it away any-more. I brought the painting up from the basement and looked that fire girl in the eyes. I futilely tried to quell the fire to a mature, reasonable, slow burn, but she couldn't compromise any longer. I have compassion for the fiery one of me because she has such conviction in not shrinking her wildness to fit inside socially sanctioned cages. She aimed to burn down anything that did not fit her absolute truth, anything that confined her to one way of being.

AUTHORITY

There were moments when forty-one felt more like fourteen, both being times when I sought any ventilation for the inner heat. I had a fairly typical rebellious phase in my late teens—drinking Bartles & Jaymes exotic berry wine coolers with friends while hiding in the sand dunes, smoking weed from dented, perforated Budweiser cans at a party when someone's parents were out of town, and having sex with my boyfriend on the couch in my parents' basement while they were asleep two floors above. Around forty-one, that defiance flared again. Of course, I replaced the wine coolers with rosé, the beer cans with a sleek one-hitter, and instead of sneaking sex while my parents were asleep, I would fantasize about having sex with a woman while my husband snored in bed beside me. When I was a teenager, my experimentation happened underground, masked by a straight-A report card and a hometown princess crown and sash. (Oh, please don't ask. Gag.) I pandered to authority— said what I was supposed to say, wore what I was told to wear, was who I was expected to be. Not anymore. Keeping my subversive nature hidden hadn't served me at all. It no longer felt like I was getting away with something, because I answered to no one.

In my forties, I began to own that I am the authority in my own life—we all are. This realization allowed me to start the quest to overturn all the introjects I swallowed as a child, the ones I explored in Chapter 3. My relationship to authority has been an ongoing learning experience. I was taught to give my power away to doctors, teachers, bosses, and even the people in my social circle. I've gained enough wisdom to begin to rework my relationship to authority in midlife. When doctors minimize symptoms even when my gut tells me that something is off, I now trust my gut. When a teacher says something that doesn't fit with what's alive in my heart, I now trust my heart. When I know I need to shift something at work that may disrupt the status quo, I trust my strong mind. When I know exactly what I need and can't stop thinking about it, despite outside messages telling me that it's bonkers, I follow my inner divine compass.

I've been undoing my own blueprints about authority the hard way. I'm slowly reclaiming my power by bringing my awareness to moments when I catch myself falling into old patterns of giving it away to others. These habits end here. I am trying to make them conscious so as not to pass them on to future generations.

TRAILBLAZING

Craig and I have taught our daughter about personal agency and consent from the get-go. Even though it's wildly unpopular in both our traditional Italian families to allow her not to hug an uncle on command, we let her make decisions about whom she makes contact with and when. It has always been in her power to choose to kiss a grandparent, and her preference is allowed to change from a "yes" in one moment to a "no" in the next. We've modeled this by asking for her permission to pick her up or to help get tangles out of her hair when she was a wee one. Asking permission is respectful and should never be awkward.

When our daughter was in grade school, Craig and I only answered the questions she asked about sex in the simplest and most developmentally appropriate way we could. Now that she's a teen, I open our talks about living in a sexual, sensual, human body to include a wider scope. These conversations may feel awkward to her at first, but they usually end with her giving me a long, silent hug where neither of us wants to let go. I want her to trust the messages her body gives her. I want her to know that there are many types of sex. I want her to know that gender and virginity are both social constructs. I want her to know that sex is pleasurable, powerful, connecting, awkward, divine, and fun. I want her to know that she is in charge of her own body and her own pleasure.

When my daughter began her period, I did the sappy, misty-eyed mom thing. I brought her both pads and tampons, and I showed her how to use them. As her menarche happened in the midst of the COVID-19 pandemic, I did not host a moon-lodge ceremony gathering in her honor, but I did collect a red bead and a written blessing from each of the key women in our circle of family and friends. I strung the beads onto a bracelet for her and created a book of the blessings, welcoming her into this next phase of her life.

Keeping a private veil over puberty and sex feels like an unhealthy and potentially dangerous approach. I reveal my own humanness and sexuality to my daughter. The fact that we are all sexual beings doesn't need to be in shadow, and in no way does it need to be in shame.

INDIVIDUATION

I believe that our souls choose the circumstances of each lifetime to work more on the curriculum we are here to master. I like to think that our souls choose our parents, our families, our environments, and that there is free will in it all. I remember attending a chakra workshop led by Caroline Myss in New York City in the early aughts where she talked about how we must be born into a family where we don't fit in order to evolve. If my hunches are true, it seems that my soul was born into a circumstance where I felt misunderstood in order to ignite the fire within me— the one that allows me to glow from within, to make myself absolutely, unapologetically visible, free, and honest. I chose a family where I felt disappointed by the lack of what I define as true intimacy so that I could do my own work in this life to foster deep, sacred bonds with others. Growing up in a system where obligation was prized lit the spark to seek absolute integrity. For this, I am grateful. In this second act of life, I've developed an allergy both to gluten and to anything that feels like constraint or obedience to rules that I did not make. Straight lines I did not draw. Boxes I did not create.

By the time I was in college, I was painfully aware that if I were to live authentically, I could not fit myself into the sweetly small and safe boxes my family of origin offered. As soon as I could break down those boxes, I tried. I instinctively decided not to move back to Virginia Beach when I graduated college at twenty, even though my entire bloodline lives there, all within a couple blocks of one another. They used to ask when I was moving back "home," but they eventually stopped. I did not venture out from my hometown to offend or avoid my dear family, but to save myself from becoming cripplingly anxious and mindlessly asleep, which is what I believed my sensitive system would have to do to adapt to that environment.

For most of my childhood, I tried so hard to fit into the relationship my mom has with my sister. Eventually, I came to accept it is completely okay that I am different, and that our individual relationships with our mom look different. In adulthood, it became clear that not only would I never catch up, but I would never fit in. Once I hit puberty and wore lip gloss, the two of them were onto other ways of connecting. I thought I was upset about being too young to read all those Judy Blume books that were kept out of reach on my bookshelf. Turns out I was feeling the first seeds of consciousness around my differences. The characteristics that make me unique, the ones that used to cause me to feel left out, are the very ones I'm leveraging in this second act of my life to heal maladaptive intergenerational patterns. As a grown woman, I've decided I never wanted to be in that cramped ladies' room at all. I may wear lip gloss, but I also swear like a fucking sailor, and I manspread when I feel like it. I don't believe in putting limitations on expression. In fact, the diversity of expression is one of the things I most relish about people.

Rainbow sheep, witch on the outskirts of the village, prodigal daughter, pariah, a woman on a heroine's (or anti-heroine's) journey—whatever I am, I chose it in an attempt to reclaim my power, to be achingly awake, and to learn to shamelessly express my truth—all of which have become lifelong pursuits that are challenging to do in any environment. It felt necessary to individuate from my family of origin so I could hear my own voice in my head over the internalized voices of my lineage. I no longer wanted to strive to be a good girl over living out my humanness. In turning my childhood messaging on its head, I've chosen to write my own rule book for my life as an adult.

SELFISH

When I had my daughter, I noticed the primary question from older generations was, "Is she an easy baby?" Growing up when and where I did, I knew precisely what this meant. It was shorthand for: "Is she quiet? Is she a doll in public? Does she acquiesce to the family's rhythm? Does she sleep through the night?" Being a difficult baby, on the other hand, would mean that she might express her needs by crying, have a tantrum in a restaurant, or wake in the middle of the night out of hunger or fear or a dirty diaper. As an adult, I engage in the ongoing work of reparenting myself until I can express my needs without feeling guilt and shame for not being "easy."

When I do anything for myself that meets my needs, or even smells remotely like self-care, I swear I can hear the chasm between me and my family of origin crack a little more. When I was in graduate school in my late twenties, I learned how to be healthily selfish—to put my needs first and to love myself foremost. We can only love another as deeply as we love ourselves. I did not want limits on my love any longer.

I used to worry about how I would be perceived by those who were still indoctrinated into the martyrdom trance I observed among the women in my family—the trance that takes pride in putting the needs of others ahead of their own. I noticed that when I engaged in my own therapy, went on a vacation, enrolled in an art class, or took a week off from work, it was often met with three little words I love to hate: "Must be nice."

"Must be nice" was such a trigger phrase for me in the past because it reminded me that I did not have the support of my family to take care of myself. It reminded me that they were judging my self-care as selfish while masking resentment or envy for not feeling free to take care of themselves. It reminded me that I grew up feeling my needs were not important, because that was a belief passed down through the women of my family for generations. I think the concept of having to set myself on fire only to keep others warm was one of the biggest lessons I had to unlearn.

DRAGON

In that pivotal forty-first year, I visited a holistic dentist to seek help for my TMJ dysfunction. I was tired of holding tightly to something between my teeth while I was sleeping; I was aching to let go. Instead of focusing on my jaw, he first diagnosed me as having a tongue tie simply by observing the way I held my neck, then he confirmed it by looking at the tightness of the little flap connecting my tongue to the bottom of my mouth, which is called the frenum. In time, I would have a frenectomy, a procedure where the frenum is "snipped" (actually, it is burned) to allow more movement. First, he said I needed to be stable enough for the procedure, as it impacted the body's midline.

I understood the significance of the midline from the perspective of having been a Waldorf/Steiner school parent. Children who attend Waldorf schools all around the world, like my daughter had, practice crossing the midline through movement and balancing exercises, bilateral art activities, and learning to knit by the end of first grade. The anthroposophical philosophy in which this type of education is grounded says this facilitates full mind-body integration before kids learn to read, as it strengthens the connection between the right and left hemispheres of the brain. My dentist knew that snipping this thread on my midline, a thread he said "holds all our shit together," could throw off the compensatory mechanisms I had developed. He warned me that, if I were unstable and unprepared, it could make bilateral coordination difficult and potentially cause a psychological break. Before he performed my first frenectomy, he required that I undergo osteopathic treatments. He cautioned that this could open a door in my life, and what I had held on to tightly would begin to loosen and flow. He provided me with case studies of former patients who had undergone this procedure and initiated major life changes afterwards, such as drastic shifts in career,

116   MIDLIFE EMERGENCE

moves to another state or country, and divorces. In addition to the physical advantage of freeing my tongue, in my restless midlife state, it was enticing to hear about the lightning bolt that might zap my life. I was sold!

Months later, magical osteopath woman, magical dentist man, and I met in his office after hours one evening for my first frenectomy. The osteopath I had been working with for about six months in preparation for this procedure laid her hands on my feet, and then my head, to determine when my energetic body was ready for the snip. I felt like a dragon, as I smelled fire and actually saw myself breathe smoke when he loosened my frenum. Moments after, the two of them watched me walk the dental office hallway to assess my coordination, like parents watching their toddler walk for the first time. We all laughed about it, but it felt like a corrective rebirth, as I opened to a new way of being in the world. Frenums tighten back to their accustomed state as they heal, so it takes a few procedures to achieve optimal results. In the two years that followed, I had three additional frenectomies under the care of this supportive team. I looked forward to each appointment. Turns out that fire breathing is quite compelling, and it set everything in motion.

REWILDING

It was just a week after my first frenectomy that I fell in love with a new form of making art—the type of art you see on the cover of this book. I took supreme pleasure in experimenting with fluid art media, as I could not easily control the process or product, nor could I create rigid or representational forms. Watching pools of color mix and harmonize on the page with seemingly accidental beauty was the antidote for the part of me who had once braced against change and held on inflexibly to pieces of myself that were begging for release. As an art therapist, I knew that specific art materials could serve as powerful healing prescriptions and that art was medicine for the soul.

By this point in my life, my spirituality and vocation had spanned into unconventional terrain—having studied transpersonal counseling and art therapy at a Buddhist university, regularly weaving energy work into my sessions, and identifying as a witch. However, my home life was close to what had been expected of me. It was quite domesticated; I was domesticated, and it had very little to do with Craig. It was self-inflicted based on my own upbringing. While in the midlife waiting room between the first and second acts of my life, mesmerized by the way my inks flowed so freely and organically in painting after painting, I felt something inside me break open. I wanted to cut all the bindings. I wanted finally to embrace my fiery feminine—not just to be rebellious but in the service of living more honestly. I didn't long to be undomesticated simply for the sake of following a trend to embrace my "wild woman archetype" or because Glennon Doyle would tell me a few years later that I needed to get untamed and be a goddamn cheetah. This desire came from deep within, not from outside. Because the yearning to unfold, unfurl, and unleash inner truth is felt among such a vast array of women in midlife, there is conversation around it in the collective. I am grateful to live in a time when women are openly talking about rewilding.

When I read the passage below, written by one of my teachers, Christiane Pelmas, it validated the personal and collective longing to reclaim our wild and to rewrite our own rules. She writes:[1]

We may be under the impression that The Burning Times are over. But women, they are as fearsome now as they ever were. Perhaps even more dangerous because so many of us have been corralled into a state of domestication. Here, we are lulled into a sense of complacency, that promises convenience but is actually a consolation. This domestication, its complacency and conciliatory strings, slowly eats away at us. For we know in our bones that our wild wisdom and fierce female voices are needed now more than ever on behalf of our children, the monarch butterflies, and the blue whale; on behalf of all Life. Rewilding ourselves is more complex than we might imagine . . . Wildness requires a state of intelligent interdependence inextricably interwoven with a fierce autonomy. We did not learn this from our mothers and grandmothers. But our well ancestral[2] women know what wild means. Together,

---

1 From https://www.christianepelmas.com/vc-3-hour-immersions/ rewilding-female-culture.

2 In ancestral work, "well ancestors" refers to those among the dead who are well in spirit who come through for guidance and healing. From Daniel Foor, https://ancestralmedicine.org/ ancestors/.

we will listen and we will speak, with our voices, our bodies, and our excavated language(s). Together, we will feed the emergent state that unfurls itself through our collective.

Each one of us has the power to create a new paradigm in which to live out the second half of life. The midlife threshold provides a vantage point where we can often see the impact that our childhood introjects have had on the identities and lives we have formed by now. We are developmentally poised during this juncture to reinvent ourselves by undergoing the individuation process yet again. This time, we are called to individuate from any social or familial messages that no longer fit for who we are becoming. We can reparent the internal, younger versions of ourselves, so that outside acceptance no longer dominates our life choices. Collectively and personally, we can restore our wild nature, the fluidity of the feminine, the right to be seen and heard, and the boundlessness of our own hearts. It won't be the same for you as it is for me, as it is for your best friend, as it is for your sister. I don't have the answers, but I do know some of the questions we can ask ourselves to begin this reclamation.

WRITE

The midlife individuation process invites us to rewrite (or completely overturn) the beliefs we received in childhood (which are called introjects) and to break the patterns that are no longer serving us. This allows our most authentic, self-expressed way of being in the world. It is self-empowerment work.

Here's your opportunity to rewrite your own rulebook to align with your updated, upleveled, adult self. Make two columns on your writing page. At the top of the page, label the left column "Introject" and label the right column "New Paradigm." On the left side of your page, under Introject, list any messages you received as a child that stick with you. Name as many as you would like, as many as flow onto the page, wanting to be brought to light. It may be helpful to revisit what you wrote from the writing prompt in Chapter 3 to refresh yourself on what you learned about needs, power, self-expression, etc.

Once you have made your introject list, use the right column to edit that introject or perhaps to turn that message completely on its head, writing the rule or message you prefer to live by going forward. For example, one of the messages in my Introject column comes from the prayers I recited every night before bed as a child: "Be a good girl." Across from this message in my New Paradigm column, the sentence reads: "Be a whole person."

CREATE

I highly recommend experimenting with wild ways of creating art. For you, that might mean tacking a giant piece of paper to your wall and make scribbling marks on it by simultaneously using jumbo crayons held in each of your fists while moving your body to whatever music makes you feel your wildness. You could also make a scribble using only your non-dominant hand. Your wild art could also involve experimenting with fluid art materials, like I did with alcohol inks for the cover of this book or with wet-on-wet watercoloring techniques. (You can look up both on the internet to find how-to videos.)

Regardless of which art supplies you choose for your wild experimentation in creation, when you are finished making a piece of art, take time to witness it. Look at the image you created from all angles. Describe what you see using "I am" statements, either out loud, in your journal, or by writing on the art itself. For example, you might say or write something like: "I am green. I am vibrant. I am tangled. I am flowing."

ALTAR RITUAL

Grab some index cards or cut up a piece of paper into small cards. Write each of the New Paradigm messages onto a card. If it feels more impactful for you to write them all on one paper, honor your intuition. You might even choose to write them on your art from the activity above, keeping it whole or cutting it into cards as you see fit. You can decorate your cards with colors or doodles, if you'd like.

Place your cards or list on your midlife emergence altar. You might choose one card per day to display on the altar. When you sit at your altar, read them to yourself and allow them to be breathed into your body, into your soul.

You are becoming more fully *you* every time you mindfully absorb these love letters to yourself.

PART II

innovation

Exploring the unfolding transformation

CHAPTER 6

looking
to the cosmos

Whatever is repressed is what Uranus will root
out, and it will tend to erupt like a volcano if
not brought to consciousness and acted on.

ELIZABETH SPRING
ASTROLOGY FOR THE THIRD ACT OF LIFE

STARGAZER

Astrology has always reoriented me to my own nature, my own brand of magic, by serving as a mirror reflecting me back to myself and validating the energies I experience. As a child, I was a stargazer, always interested in the impact of the heavens on our earthly bodies and souls. I began to study astrology when I was about eleven, though I never mastered it as a vocation.

Even if you don't follow astrology, you can probably feel that humans are as tidal as the ocean, as we are made mostly of water and are undeniably affected by the pull of the moon. Although the moon may be the closest celestial body to us here, she has a lot of powerful planetary neighbors who also weigh in on what is playing out down here on Earth. As industrialized as we have become, we cannot deny our connection to the cosmos and to our wild animal nature.

When I was twenty-nine years old, a dear friend referred me to an amazing, progressive astrologer named Eric Meyers, with whom I've consulted on every birthday since. Here I was, nearing my forty-second birthday, desperately afraid that my fiery longing might change everything. The faster I had run from the hot irritability over that year, the more I fanned those flames, and the brighter they burned inside. As my birthday approached, I scheduled my annual astrology reading with Eric, wondering what sort of dance those faraway celestial bodies might be doing, to be pushing, pulling, and igniting me in this particularly uncomfortable way.

URANUS
December 2017

On the day of my session, I closed myself in my home office, lit a candle, and got on a call with Eric. He told me I was nearing the peak of a passage called the Uranus opposition, which is astrology-speak for what's been known as the "midlife crisis." On an astrology chart, the active human life span is regarded as eighty-four years, which is the amount of time it takes for Uranus to revolve around our sun. Therefore, in astrology, midlife is said to peak at age forty-two, when Uranus has traversed 180 degrees, or halfway across the zodiac, from the position where it was at the time of our birth. The Uranus opposition, this midway point, is an astrological event that gets less press in modern pop culture than a Mercury retrograde or the Saturn return, but it is a comparable planetary occurrence. It usually hits its exact (screaming) midpoint when we are around age forty-two, so we are likely to feel the effects of it for a couple years on either side of that age.

Eric got quite excited as we talked, as he was already making connections between what I described in my life and the energy that the Uranus opposition stirs up. He explained to me that Uranus is the planet of rebellion, freedom, unpredictability, and higher awareness. It teaches us how we can find true inner freedom through rejecting what does not serve us. The Uranus opposition offers us this pause wherein we can shift our identification from the expectations of childhood to a more mature expression of the self. He said that Uranus is like a good friend who calls us on our bullshit, as it blows open anything that has felt held back or repressed once it reaches this passage. If we have not made visible what we've kept invisible by the time we hit our forties, Uranus will invite us to take action and create change. The invitations may just nag at us like irritable, agitated, unmet longings, or they could create volcanic explosions in our lives. Regardless of their magnitude, these eruptions can feel shocking and unexpected—not only from the inside, but also to those witnessing us.

When we move through the Uranus opposition, the energy can be intense, calling us to course-correct and move into greater alignment with our purpose and truth. We are invited to shift from the self we may have acquired as a survival strategy growing up to the self who reflects the entirety of our being. According to Eric, this midlife passage is when we have an opportunity to graduate from our spiritual childhood into our spiritual adulthood. It's a time of rebelling against limitations imposed by our families, our society, and ourselves. Even though we will all experience another potent astrological transit close to age fifty-nine, during the Uranus opposition at forty-two, we may feel an urgency around beginning this shift. In my case, I experienced a pressing need to muster the courage to emerge as more whole and as more myself.

LUNAR

I explained to Eric that I was constantly grappling with how I could satisfy my unmet longing (to live in the fullness of my sexuality) while still upholding the integrity of the life to which I had committed. He offered a way that astrology could provide a clue as to the flavor of my soul's purpose, which involved studying the astrological lunar nodes. The lunar nodes are the points where the moon's orbit pierced through the ecliptic plane (the imaginary map of the Earth's orbit around the sun) in the northern and southern hemispheres when we were born. He explained to me that we each have a north and south node, both of which are in a particular zodiac sign and correspond to a particular house in astrology. The lunar nodes will always be polar opposites on the zodiac wheel that depicts the twelve astrological signs. Some astrologers refer to the lunar nodes as "the dragon in your chart," with the head pointed to the north node and the tail to the south. I thought to myself, "Oooh, there's the fire breather again."

Eric taught me that the south node represents the karmic past and has the feeling of a third-grade maturity level. I learned that in astrology, the south node is an energetic bucket of relationships, habits, situations, and karma from past lifetimes that we are here in this lifetime to resolve, as well as gifts we are here to carry forward. When we read about the sign of our south node, it is likely to feel like a comfort zone, but it isn't necessarily spicy or exciting.

The north node gives a clue as to our soul's mission for further expansion, as the soul reaches toward fully mature self-governance. Eric said the north node points to the area of massive growth potential for our souls. When we hear about the qualities of our own north nodes, we may get a sense of awe, excitement, reverence, and perhaps intimidation. This is the definition of the Hebrew word *yirah*, a feeling I had been chasing all year.

In my forty-second birthday astrology reading, I learned that my south node is in Taurus in the seventh house, which, in plain English, means that I've been seeking structure, acceptance, and approval (Taurus) in relationships (seventh house), which has amplified my tendencies to people-please and conform to the status quo. This tracks with my lifelong tendency to defer to the preferences of others—to be the sweet, peacemaking, good girl. My north node is in Scorpio in the first house, which means my growing edge is toward intensity, freedom, sexuality, passion, depth, empowerment, risk, and intimacy (Scorpio) in my identity and approach to life (first house).

Eric let me know that my Uranus opposition (which I was already calling my midlife emergence) was inviting me to be fierce in liberating parts of myself that had felt confined to a soul cage of security and comfort. I had been amenable to that cage and making the best of it because the social norms pointed me toward what I "should" have been doing. Karmically, all that should-ing had created a wild, fiery freedom impulse over the years, which could not help but come flying out of the cage in my midlife emergence, wings spread wider than they had ever expanded before.

My immediate (and somewhat rebelliously adolescent) reaction was to move away from my karmic past and leap into the bold evolution that my north node promised. It made so much sense, given the itch I had been feeling and the unconventional themes I had been exploring. Eric paused me there and cautioned me about my interpretation. He told me that, in his view, the mission is *not* simply to move completely away from the south node's qualities while growing toward the north node; rather, it is to expand into the north node's invitation while *integrating* it into the karma of the south node, always in the service of wholeness. We are leveraging our south node strengths while moving into north node territory in order to become more integrated. So, for me, this means I am to follow my own truth, however unpopular, while remaining in connected relationship to others.

Living into this high end of my chart, or following the dragon's trajectory for my soul's path, felt scary on the days when I just wanted to accept the good-enoughness of my life, the days when I lacked the gusto to make changes.

I sometimes wanted to curl into a blanket with all my familiar south-node habits. Yet, the pull toward expansion into
those intense, passionate, unknown realms became so
seductive that I couldn't ignore their force any longer.

PURPOSE

In that astrology reading with Eric, I listened with quiet
tears streaming down my face. He had affirmed my hunch
that my purpose is to take as many edgy risks as possible
in the service of my soul's growth toward radical self-
alignment. I cried because I knew the risk I would have to
face, and I was not ready.

I often think back to one specific remark Eric made in
that session: "You are here in this lifetime to risk getting
more wounded. Some people come into this life very
wounded, and they're here to chill out. You're here to
risk pushing the envelope a lot more." Eric went on to
tell me that my soul's intention is to teach and normalize ideas that are, as he put it, "more witchy, woo-woo,
shamanic, taboo, sexual, intimate, edgy, deep, sacred,
liberated, and unconventional." (I experience a full-body,
full-soul "YES!" to these words each time I read them.) My
astrology says that my midlife emergence is an initiation
into expansion, making my own map and rules, honoring spicier intimate desires, going more deeply into
truth, challenging tradition and structure, and fiercely
claiming my freedom. My astrology also points to a lot
of specifics around overturning the convention of how
marriage should look, and it even reveals themes of
sexual intimacy with women. It always astounds me how

what we're up to here on Earth is so clearly reflected in the cosmos.

For someone with my history and personality, growing toward my soul's full potential has me shaking in my fuzzy slippers as I sit here at my desk, writing my story with the intention to share it with the world. Simultaneously, it makes my belly flip with excitement to be taking a step toward who I am meant to become. To be visible in the messy truth of my life is a tall order for someone whose soul has sought approval and acceptance for lifetimes, but this growth is what my dragon's head is aiming toward. Nothing feels more important to me than using the themes Eric unveiled about my own life path as a way to support the healing experience of others. Astrology can validate for us what we're already doing and noticing. It also assured me that standing in my truth and sharing openly in this body of work could inspire you, dear reader, to claim your own truth.

The midlife emergence wakes us up to the ticking clock. We might sense an urgency to experience it all, as well as the knowing that we could not have arrived in this place of readiness without having traversed each moment along the way. It's all in right timing.

Our lunar nodes can provide a clue about the unmet longing or unexpressed facet of identity that is deeply yearning to unfurl as we enter the Uranus opposition or traverse the midlife passage. That fire-breathing dragon in the sky can offer us a map and a mirror for this fire-breathing time of life. Understanding our astrological transits can feel like an endorsement from the cosmos to trust what we already know deep inside. Many of us have only been following guides prescribed by patriarchy or by our lineage, and now it is time to take the helm of our own beautifully divine ships as they sail through space and time. It's frightening. It's exhilarating. And it's simply all there is to do.

RESEARCH

Understanding your own astrology, particularly your lunar nodes, may shed some moonlight on what your soul is here to do. The south node will give you information about the karmic ties you are healing, your natural abilities, and your comfort zone. Your north node will provide clues into the higher destiny that would be fulfilling to move toward.

Even if you don't consult with an astrologer, you can easily find your own north and south nodes online. There are several free astrology websites that will provide this information. Simply do a search like: "What are my north and south nodes in astrology?" This will bring up a choice of websites where you will enter your birth date, birth time, and birth city. From there, the site will provide your natal chart, which will display information about your north and south nodes. Once you know the signs of your nodes, you can do a deeper dive by searching something like—to use mine as an example—"North node Scorpio" and "South node Taurus," which will offer you more information about where you've been and where you're headed. If you prefer to get an astrological reading, be sure to ask about your north and south nodes to gain insight into your soul's work at this juncture.

WRITE

Grab your writing materials of choice. Write down the sign and house of your north and south nodes, and whatever characteristics you learned from your research.

Now, set a timer for three minutes. Free-write for the entire three minutes (or more, if you have more to say) without letting your pen stop moving. Write any feelings, memories, or associations that arise regarding what you are discovering about your lunar nodes and how they might apply to your midlife emergence.

CREATE

You may have created a vision board before, but this invitation is specific to your lunar nodes. You might even wish to cut a piece of poster board or large paper into the shape of a dragon to use as your backdrop. Then, flip through magazines, old photos, or memorabilia and cut out anything that corresponds to what you've learned about your south and north nodes. You may also wish to peruse the internet and print out photos or words for your collage.

Next, arrange the images onto your poster board. If you're using the shape of a dragon, you may want to arrange the south node images near the tail and the north node images near the head. If you're using a square or rectangle, perhaps you place the south node associations near the bottom and the north node associations near the top or organize them in a way that allows you to see their polarity, envisioning how you might bridge that into an integrated continuum. Because our astrology invites us to unify the comforts of the south node with the newness of the north node, this activity will help you to view them as whole and connected, and hopefully, you will be able to see yourself reflected in the finished image.

ALTAR RITUAL

Locate an object or image that represents the qualities of what you learned from your research about your south node. Remember, your south node is what you've historically found comforting and easy for you; it also represents the past ties you are aiming to heal during this time. Place the object or image on the left side of your altar.

Find an item or image that represents the energy of your particular north node. Your north node represents the high end of your soul's purpose, or what you have the potential to evolve into. Place the object or image on the right side of your altar. Light the candle and sit quietly at your altar space to integrate this new piece of insight.

CHAPTER 7

walking the tightrope

It takes a lot of courage to release the familiar and seemingly secure, to embrace the new. But there is no real security in what is no longer meaningful. There is more security in the adventurous and exciting, for in movement there is life, and in change there is power.

ALAN COHEN *JOY IS MY COMPASS*

TABOOS

In my astrology reading, Eric explained the crossroads in which I found myself by telling me which planet was in which sign under which house. It had something to do with my Juno and Gemini and other things that were beyond the scope of my astrology prowess. Then he exclaimed, "Two taboos! Being queer and polyamorous!" When I heard this, something inside me, where I was storing a boatload of internalized oppression, shuddered and wanted to hide. He followed that exclamation with a sincere "Congratulations!" He told me that if I were to engage in the soul growth my midlife emergence offered, or in his words, if I were to "do the midlife passage well, the way life looked before and after crossing this threshold would be completely different." The straight-A geek in me wanted to "do it well" and get the A+, so apparently I accepted the invitation.

There are some very key childhood introjects that I'm working to address in midlife—the unspoken rules I followed around my sexuality and my relationship status. I wished to heal a lifetime of toxic monogamy messaging that had caused me to be bound in my own expressions of intimacy. I hoped to learn a new way to work with my intense jealousy when my partners expressed attraction or attention toward someone other than myself. I also aimed to reconcile a lifetime of suppressing my desire for a female lover.

It was time for my sexuality to have a channel for expression, but I strongly preferred for it not to rock my stable family life. I didn't want to choose between the weight of my heart's longstanding commitments and the groundspeed of novel rapture. For that reason, my and Craig's experiment with ethical non-monogamy felt like a smart, creative way for us to have it all. For a woman like me, who had been acting out intergenerational wounds and "good girl" appearances in all her adult relationships, this was a bold move.

TEAM

Craig and I made an amazing team. After almost two decades together, we had partnership and co-adulting down to a science, divvying up the household and parenting duties, as well as the earning and caretaking roles. We knew whose week it was to grocery shop and whose week it was to do the laundry. It was obvious that I did the shopping for clothing, decor, and birthday gifts, while Craig kept us stocked in toilet paper, batteries, and filters for air vents. Craig booked our travel, and I packed our bags. We had a whiteboard in the kitchen detailing all our dinners for the week, and we shopped for the ingredients on Sundays. In the year before our move to Boulder, at the top of that whiteboard, Craig had written a reminder for us that we did not erase. It was a manifesto of this new phase together. In all caps, it read: BREAK ALL PATTERNS.

When it came to relocating our family, Craig and I operated like a well-oiled machine. As a Sagittarius with true wanderlust spirit, I have moved quite often. As I write this, I am sitting at my desk, directly downstairs from the twenty-sixth bedroom I've had in my life, twenty-one of which I've occupied during adulthood, most of those shared with Craig. We have successfully completed searches for apartments in New York City; Boulder, Colorado; Richmond, Virginia; and all over the San Francisco Bay Area. We bought a gorgeous home together in Virginia, and now we were doing the same in Colorado.

NEST
Spring/Summer 2018

This move back to Boulder was no different in the way we divided and conquered. He focused on holding down the fort by making sure his job would still be secure after our move as well as watching our daughter when I traveled to Colorado to set up our new life. I flew to Colorado often to manage a renovation project involving new appliances, countertops, tile, light fixtures, paint, flooring, etc. I was making the perfect forever nest for our family in the city I most adored, cozied up close to my nearest and dearest friends.

That spring, I mostly traveled to our new home state without my family, and I enjoyed time with friends on these visits. They would leave their children with their partners so we could party like we did in graduate school. I felt my younger, more social self re-emerge. It occurred to me that over the past decade in California, I had not been around my closest friends very often in the company of my daughter, and I seldom saw them when I was with Craig. I was feeling more and more split between this wilder, more independent version of me and the domestic, mom/wife. I became nervous about the adjustment it would take to weave those parts of myself together once my family moved to Colorado.

On my last solo visit to Boulder that June, just five days before we would move into our new house as a family, I looked around the empty, pristine space with pure satisfaction. It felt perfect. I was so proud of us. During our twenty-year relationship, we had gone through periods of unemployment, debt, and food stamps. As a team, we worked our way back to a place where we could buy a house, send our child to a private school, and have savings accounts. This house felt like a symbol of Craig's professional accomplishments and my commitment to tending to details that reflected the love, care, and beauty I wanted to give my family every day.

I walked around the xeriscaped front yard of our new home, noticing the bursting of all the resplendent, native flowers. I noted the many rose bushes and remembered our wedding ceremony, during which the officiant had invited us to keep a small vase in our home where we would offer a rose to one another after any conflict, as a reminder of our enduring love. For whatever reason, that particular ritual from our wedding never stuck. However, in my guilt and gratitude for getting what I wanted in moving us all to Boulder, I had the urge to make a giant vase of homegrown roses for him.

MARRIAGE

Craig and I were married on the summer solstice of 2003. In our ceremony, we vowed this to each other: "In the presence of the divine, I take you to be my beloved spiritual partner, to affirm the truth of your being in every moment, to love, to honor, to cherish, to tenderly care for you, to support and nurture your fulfillment through all the changes of our life. I promise you this from my heart with all my being, for all the days of my life. And beyond the walls of life and the bounds of time." I remember feeling the sweet gravity of that declaration at the altar noticeably change my cellular structure. It comforted me then and, honestly, it still does. On our wedding day, this vow was immediately followed by Craig's smart-ass uncle shouting from the audience, "Whoa! You sure, Craig? That's a big promise!" It was. And we were sure.

Summer solstice, our wedding day, is the day with the longest stretch of daylight, as the sun has grown to its full strength, and the days begin to get shorter from there. It's the annual equivalent of the monthly full moon. Midsummer, or the summer solstice, has been known to be a day for lovers, yin energy, eros, passion, wildness, and sensuality. It's a pagan holiday celebrated by a fire festival to symbolize the heat of the summer sun, a day to honor the generous, divine mother goddess, and a day to honor fathers who plant the seed of life. It's a bittersweet holiday that reminds us that nothing lasts forever, that the light must fade, and we must let go once something is complete. It reminds us that the temporal nature of all of life makes it that much more precious. It reminds us to be grateful in the moment, to love with our whole hearts, and to express that love while we can. When we let go, we allow something to change and grow.

This is how Craig and I continue to honor the wedding vows we took on the solstice all those years ago. We allow each other to evolve and hold the freest versions of each other in complete love. A passage from Anne Morrow Lindbergh's book *Gift from the Sea*—read by a friend during our wedding ceremony—expresses this attitude:

A good relationship has a pattern like a dance and is built on some of the same rules. The partners do not need to hold on tightly, because they move confidently in the same pattern, intricate but gay and swift and free, like a country dance of Mozart's. To touch heavily would be to arrest the pattern and freeze the movement, to check the endlessly changing beauty of its unfolding. There is no place here for the possessive clutch, the clinging arm, the heavy hand; only the barest touch in passing. Now arm in arm, now face to face, now back to back—it does not matter which. Because they know they are partners moving to the same rhythm, creating a pattern together, and being invisibly nourished by it. The joy of such a pattern is not only the joy of creation or the joy of participation, it is also the joy of living in the moment. Lightness of touch and living in the moment are intertwined.

Craig's name literally means "crag dweller," like one who dwells alone in a cave, and it suits him—not only because he is an introverted, hermit type, but because in our marriage, Craig was the stable rock to my dancing fire. He kept the ground steady while I explored freely. This was a profound gift of our relationship, yet it was also a pattern we acknowledged we needed to break. It was one that kept me feeling disempowered, dependent, and dissatisfied while I feared Craig was storing up a mountain of resentment as he sacrificed his whims so I could indulge mine.

When I married Craig at twenty-seven years old, after our nearly four-year courtship, I already knew I did not want traditional gender roles to play out in my marriage in the way I had seen them modeled in my family. I had swung far in the opposite direction of my mother, who is the ultimate keeper of home. I still have visions of coming home from elementary school to find her thanklessly ironing while watching *General Hospital* in the living room. Reflexively, in my own marriage, we divvied up the household chores quite differently. And (gasp!) we didn't own an iron.

Even before we married, I was uninterested in becoming a "good wife." If something smelled even the least bit obligatory, I didn't do it. If the word *should* was attached, I would run the other way. The feelings of doing what I wanted and getting what I wanted were such a missing piece (read: gaping mother-effing hole) from my childhood that the allure of self-sovereignty was irresistible.

In the years before we got married, we grappled with complex jealousy issues, but the solutions we found were neither healthy nor sustainable. When we met, we bonded through a playful friendship in which we checked out women together. We would be sitting at a bar in New York City, a few cocktails in, talking about nearby women, getting to know each other's types. In our early friendship, I was also made aware of his indiscretions in all his prior relationships. Once we began dating each other exclusively, our open sharing about other women changed radically. When Craig would show any appreciation of other women, it ignited my jealous programming. I feared that our pasts would predict our future, meaning that I was terrified he would secretly cheat and leave me for someone else. Given what I had observed in my parents' divorce and the infidelity I had endured in previous relationships, I felt rashly threatened when Craig even looked at another woman.

Understandably, just a couple years into our courtship, Craig grew tired of fighting for his autonomy in this way. His solution was to lock away parts of his own sexual being to appease me, because he did not want to lose me and because we were in our early twenties with less sophisticated relational skills. We fought whenever any of his ex-girlfriends came up in conversation, so eventually we stopped talking about them. He essentially put blinders on himself. I truly did not know the level of self-restraint he was employing until he told me during our midlife talks about opening our marriage. He admitted that he not only kept it to himself when he saw an attractive woman but, to avoid a fight, he would also choose to seat himself in a restaurant where he faced the wall so as not to be tempted to look. I wondered how much of this behavior was even conscious for him. When we stopped arguing about jealousy in our twenties, from my vantage point at the time, I figured he had simply matured and was ready for "a real commitment" because he had found "the right person." I felt so grateful to be with someone so devoted, who spoke to my core desire to be special and chosen. I have had to work through so much shame about these ugly parts of myself hooking perfectly into those vulnerable parts of Craig. I've stomached a load of regret for the repercussions this had on our relationship—tangles and knots we would later try desperately to untie.

Four years into our marriage, we had our daughter. The first year of her life was difficult for us both. After a fairly traumatic cesarean birth and a subsequent stretch of arduous healing, we felt like we were in survival mode. The amount of time and freedom we each lost when she was born was a rude awakening for which we were sorely unprepared. We teased ourselves for not knowing how selfish we were with our time until we had a child. We were resentful toward each other when one of us got a slice of time away from parenting. For me, time away meant two hours at most between breastfeeding sessions for a shower and maybe a snack or a phone call. Craig's time away was almost entirely spent working or doing household chores. Around her first birthday, we learned we were parenting a child with a life-threatening food allergy. The anxiety of keeping our child alive ate up pretty much all my cortisol and obliterated my libido. I kept my head down in parenthood for a solid decade, with the buzzing anxiety of keeping this little human alive. I barely even talked to friends on the phone during my daughter's waking hours in her early years.

Becoming parents cracked our hearts wide open in a way I cannot imagine anything else on this planet doing. It taught me about love in a way I could not have experienced otherwise. Yet, in all the attachment parenting and my vicious postpartum anxiety, I lost key parts of my passion and fire. Their juicy magenta and blazing orange colors were absolutely drained from my exhausted body.

Around the time our daughter was ten, something in me seemed to thaw out, crack open, and pour forth with fervor. I have noticed a trend among my friends and clients who are parents that the eldest child's tenth birthday seems to be a pivotal point, in that both parent and child are beginning a parallel process of finding independence from one another. As soon as my daughter turned ten, it was as though the sensual aspect of my being came back online full force. I listened to my own music again in the car instead of Kimya Dawson's *Alphabutt* album. I danced alone in my art studio. I craved foods I had enjoyed before becoming a mom.

I felt the lightning spark of sexual desire again in my body—only it was entirely for women. Craig and I were having connected and loving sex, though not as frequently as he would have liked and more frequently than I felt authentically stirred. This was the beginning of our conversations about attempting ethical non-monogamy to accommodate my reawakened yearning.

OPENING

I didn't want to shrink myself to fit into a box of social norms around sexuality or relationship definitions. At the time, a conventional type of life (and a conventional type of love) felt too small for my ever-expanding heart. I wanted to find a way of self-governance with compassion and honesty. For me and for Craig, the idea of ethical non-monogamy felt like it offered a brilliant solution, however unconventional.

The fact that Craig and I were willing to open our marriage likely looked ludicrous from the outside. To our friends and families, we were known as the couple who was deeply in love and could work through anything. They could have never imagined the material we were currently working through behind closed doors. We saw consensual non-monogamy as an inventive way to address the situation presented to us. We felt we had three choices:

1 Repress my sexuality forever and keep our jealousy patterns where they were, which might result in our living in resentment until we died.

2 Cheat on one another, which would undoubtedly lead to more deeply carved jealousy wounds and a bitter divorce.

3 Open the marriage and our communication with each other so that we could evolve our souls and experience the fullness of their expressions in this life, with absolute freedom and unconditional love.

Clearly, we chose the third path. When we moved to Boulder, I hadn't had the opportunity to be with anyone else sexually or romantically. Craig still didn't want to seek out another partner for himself, and Emily, my utterly heart-crushing crush of a best friend, was unavailable. Craig and I had told our friends about our new arrangement; some of them were concerned and others were supportive, but both of us had far too much indoctrination and shame to tell our families. Besides, the rubber hadn't yet hit the road. At this point, our open marriage was theoretical. We read a lot. We talked a lot. We went slowly. We felt empowered in that we would get to decide what our version of this would look like.

In all our talking, I eventually and reluctantly agreed that the openness could be reciprocal. I decided this *not* because I felt like I could suddenly be magically chill with the idea of Craig being with another woman. That was definitely *not* the case. I hoped it would be freeing for my soul. In many ways, an open marriage sounded like homeopathy, when a disease is treated with minute doses of a drug that would produce in a healthy person symptoms similar to those of the disease. In other words, this experiment would be a version of my having a hair-of-the-jealousy-dog that bit me. It made sense to us that by being with other people, we might be able to heal the jealousy that had permeated our marriage and created a restricted pattern. We thought this would be safe if we did it consciously, with much respect, love, support, and communication. It felt like it could help us to heal the imbalanced power dynamic. Non-monogamy seemed like an adequate solution for achieving more expansion and freedom while keeping our family intact. We hoped this arrangement could potentially give me a corrective experience around having my needs matter as well as repair the feeling that they would never be met.

We also felt that our open marriage would serve to model the idea that love and intimacy could be more expansive and diverse than the sanctioned confines of monogamous marriage. It could abolish this socially constructed binary between friendship and romantic love. In a grand sense, we hoped it would help heal intergenerational restrictions backward and forward throughout time and space.

I was ready to tear down the walls I had built around my heart. Once Craig and I opened ourselves to the idea that we would venture into this together, I immediately felt my heart expand and the container widen. I felt more whole, more full, more loving. I felt committed to helping Craig's sensual nature break free and to support him in taking the blinders off. I loved him enough to want him to be free, even if that meant it would be difficult at times, even if that meant he wouldn't choose me every time. I knew it would break my egoic heart, but not the heart of my higher self.

I saw this as a clear opportunity to heal my jealousy in a non-theoretical way, to grow myself enough to face the darker parts of me. It would challenge me to quiet the inner voice of my mother, perpetuating the insecurity and people-pleasing. That way of being is not inherently mine; it was imprinted from a time long before me. It was tattooed into my birthmarks and my thumbprints and my heartbeat. For decades, I had worked so hard in therapy to free myself from those automatic thought patterns, though the true test had yet to come.

At the start of opening our relationship, the deal Craig and I made was to bring each other along into our individual experiences. We promised to share our joys, excitements, and hardships so we wouldn't find ourselves on divergent paths. The intention was to bring everything to each other so we could share and grow *together*. This in no way would diminish or downplay the connection we might have for our other lovers. We intended to prioritize our marriage and parenting, which felt like a natural path for our particular circumstance. Deconstructing the well-carved concept of marriage might be a messy shitshow, but we were signing up for it all. Eyes wide open.

The bigger systemic issue behind any hesitancy I have to share my story is that, in our society, non-monogamy is even more closeted and shame-laden than homosexuality. It's time to shine light on the fact that these relationships exist and are valid. I want to live in a world where no one feels the need to pretend they live or love in a way other than the way they actually do. I hope that the cultural shift occurring now means that generations coming up can feel safe and open to exploring ideologies outside of what's been expected and decide which types of relationship dynamics work for each person. Being visible in non-monogamy can heal the binary way people view this world, the way our culture has shut down around how relationships, intimacy, and marriage need to look. I wanted to be a part of the emergent edge that is shifting and widening these views, creating a new paradigm propelled by our birthright for pleasure and many flavors of love. The only way I could overcome my shame about a lifestyle so divergent from the way I was raised was to keep reminding myself that what we were embarking upon was deeply good for me, healing for Craig, valuable for our daughter, and evolutionary for our culture.

During our first year back in Colorado, I made up for lost time socially. I had missed my Boulder community for the thirteen years since graduating from Naropa, and I was elated to be neighbors again. I went out to teas, brunches, lunches, dinners, and cocktails with my girlfriends several times a week. Craig and I would sometimes go on double dates with friends who were coupled and arrange play-dates with families who had kids our daughter's age. We had big birthday parties and intimate dinner parties in our beautiful new home. In our marriage, we joked that it was my duty to make friends in each city where we lived and to maintain those friendships through planning all the social activities. Planning, gathering, and being the connective tissue in my friend groups was one of my superpowers. Craig wasn't nearly as interested in meeting people or planning get-togethers, and he often preferred his alone time while I went out. Once we were back in Boulder, I saw old, familiar, beloved parts of myself resurface. I laughed more often, I sang in my car, and I attended ecstatic-dance gatherings. In this time, I also felt the truth of my queerness emerging more fully, and I felt haunted by it.

URGENCY
May 2019

We had been in our new home for almost a year when I found myself discussing with my therapist my deep-rooted shame for not living in a way that was fully congruent with my sexuality. I immediately experienced a strong wave of nausea—a heavy, murky discomfort in my gut. Feeling disempowered and small, I curled up into a ball in the upholstered armchair across from her. The chakra-nerd in me recognized that the gut is the third chakra, the solar plexus, corresponding to our digestive organs and how we not only process our food but also process emotional content. The third chakra houses our personal power, will, and self-esteem. The shadow side of the third chakra is none other than that pesky feeling of shame. The nausea passed as I drove home after the therapy session. Over the next couple days, each time I journaled and talked with close friends about this shame, I sensed that same familiar wave of nausea.

A few mornings later, when the moon was full, Craig rushed me to the hospital with the worst stomachache of my life. Within the hour, I underwent an emergency appendectomy. Just before the doctor put me under, I had an opportunity to go to the bathroom. I remember looking at my aging face in the mirror under that sterile, cold bathroom light. This was a reckoning moment where I realized that life is fucking short. I vowed that if I lived through the surgery (yeah, I'm a little dramatic when I'm terrified), I would fully commit to the process of turning myself inside out until I was integrated enough not to notice the difference. As a team of nurses prepped me for surgery and administered the relaxation medications through my IV, Craig held my hand while I cried to him about parts of life I had yet to live. Slipping into a medicated state, I whined out loud, "I haven't even had sex with a woman yet!" Craig squeezed my hand and promised me that we would make all of that happen and that he would always be there. As entertaining as that scene may have been to the nurses, the mortal urgency and his support that day were a call to action for me.

While there are medical reasons for having an emergency appendectomy, the psychosomatics of such an ailment can be profoundly meaningful. The fact that it happened on a full moon, which is a monthly time we witches use for rituals to release that which is no longer aligned, felt auspicious. Energetically, appendicitis can mean that one is blocking the natural flow of life, and, at the time, I was still desperately bolstering against the precarious dam that protected everything I knew.

FEAR

Even though the human nervous system is programmed to keep us safe, we also crave venturing into the unknown in service of evolution, growth, and change. To me, Craig's and my consensual non-monogamy arrangement felt like the compromise between the safety of our familiar, secure home life and the thrill of investigating new and exciting terrain. In midlife, the question naturally becomes how to balance our penchant for the security of a familiar homeostasis with exploring the prospect of how we might expand and unfold by traversing uncertainty. This was the tightrope I walked.

When I review the fear-based choices I've made in my life in order to stay safe, it's the only time I really experience regret. For example, when I was seventeen, I began college at Virginia Tech. Even though I graduated in the top one percent of my high school class, affording me a broad choice of amazing universities, I applied for early admission to a general state school for two reasons that were merely about safety: 1) it was in-state, thus close to home, and 2) my older sister Kim had gone to college there, so it felt familiar. I chose Virginia Tech by default and purely out of fear.

Once freshman year began, I felt depressed, alone, uninspired, and invisible there on a giant, ice-storm-ridden campus in the Blue Ridge Mountains. I never felt like I belonged at such a large university, in such huge, anonymous auditorium classrooms. I never belonged at football games, at sorority meetings, at fraternity parties. I would walk from my dorm to my classes across the drill field every weekday, wiping my tears as they froze on my lashes from the bitter cold. I was sick my entire freshman year, constantly popping damaging antibiotics from the school infirmary while living in a teeny dorm room. I considered transferring, but I had never quit or made a major shift at that point in my life, and no one I knew supported such a path. The approval of those around me held a lot of weight back then.

Nothing about the three and a half years (I graduated early to get the fuck outta there) I spent at Tech felt congruent with who I was, and it was the lowest point of my life to date. Instead of higher education, career prep, or learning how to do my own laundry, the most valuable lesson I got out of my undergraduate studies was: *Never choose something only because it seems safe.*

When I've chosen the safer path, it has generally left me feeling stuck in someone else's idea of who I am rather than my own. After that undergraduate experience, I got better at saying no to what's not for me and yes to my unique, inner voice with her offbeat ideas. Through this, I learned that when something is growth-producing, it can also feel scary. And we can do it anyway. We can absolutely do it scared.

FORWARD

In this midlife transition, we walk a precarious edge between who we've been and who we are to become. During my midlife emergence, I felt like a tightrope walker, just stepping her toes out onto the very thin line connecting these two identities. Abraham Maslow said, "In any given moment we have two options: to step forward into growth or to step back into safety." (Oof, let that one sink in.)

Sometimes we mistake safety for happiness. During times when I have felt small, insecure, exhausted, or even just particularly nostalgic, I've wanted to retreat to base, convincing myself that having had my pinky toe on that highwire for a moment was satisfying enough. That's when the internalized shoulds have crept up, encouraging me to stay secure, to stuff down all my desires, to put away my needs, and to just be grateful for what I already had, because it was damn good. Other times, I have found myself up there in a sequined rainbow catsuit and on absolute fucking fire—dying to skip, leap, and cartwheel across that highwire, seeking more growth, more freedom, more me. The tightrope was so long that I couldn't even see the platform on the other side. I wondered, *Is it there? Is it stable? Will loved ones be there to greet me on the other side?*

The thing is, when we're in an audience, watching a tightrope walker do her thing, we hold our breath when she walks across, way up high, and we cheer when she makes it! If she were to go back to the starting platform, never taking the second step, climbing back down the ladder, and walking out of the ring, we would be let down. When it's not a circus performer but someone we love dearly, we are often more comforted (and maybe we even cheer) when we see her safe and secure, where we *expect* her to be, who she has always been to us. When we get to witness a loved one taking a risk, stepping forward into the mystery and unknown, we get flustered and out of sorts. Maybe we have mistaken our worry for love. Or maybe it makes us question our own lives and choices, wondering (perhaps with unconscious envy) if we could ever be so bold as to go find out what's on the other side of our own tightropes. I've been there and have felt those feelings for my loved ones. I've been the audience member hiding my eyes, the steady spotter down below, the one with arms spread wide waiting on the platform on the other side. And in the midst of midlife, I found myself the daring, frightened, rapturous tightrope walker, ready to step out.

As we age, we become more aware of the momentum of energy that flows through life—how there's a quickening that's seductive to follow. We have free will to choose whether to take the risk of shaking things up. If we resist, we often stay safe and maintain the life we've lived. If we say yes to the opportunity, we could get hurt, and we will certainly end up somewhere new.

In midlife, not only did I become a person who saw these opportunity threads, but I almost couldn't forgo their pull anymore. I learned to surrender to this flow, and to get really curious about what wanted to happen, even as my whole being shook, making my tightrope wobble.

WRITE

Your tightrope is the string between your absolutely familiar, safe homeostasis and the unfamiliar, enticing mystery. If you're in your midlife passage and reading this book, you're likely able to relate to the tightrope walker, and you're balancing somewhere along this seemingly precarious wire. Here are some journaling questions to consider:

- What does it look like on the starting platform, in the safe familiar of your life?

- What is your tightrope cord made of? How supportive and dependable is it?

- Who is watching you? Are the spectators cheering, gasping, or silently covering their eyes?

- What's the feeling in your belly when you take bold steps toward the unknown? What happens when you lose your balance?

- What do you think you might be moving toward? What might be waiting for you on the other side of the platform, even if you can't see it? What are you afraid

it might be? In your wildest fantasies,
what do you hope it might be?

CREATE

As you brave your own personal tightrope, it can
be useful to have a talisman to remind you of your
inner anchor of safety. You can use any materials
you like to create a symbol of your own personal
safe place. To create this place, imagine what your
inner resources are around safety. Perhaps they
have to do with your health, your savings account,
a few trusted friends, your faith. You can collage
or draw these things. Maybe your safe place elicits
a feeling of being cozy or enveloped in softness.
You could find a small box and put items in it that
evoke these feelings of safety for you when you see
or touch them. It could be that an object or piece
of jewelry you'll wear reminds you of your internal
safe place. Bring yourself into frequent contact
with that object during this time.

ALTAR RITUAL

Use an object you discovered in the exercise
above that represents what is safe and secure for
you. Also, find an object that reflects the mystery
of what unfolds before you. You may wish to find
something that symbolizes your journey from
known to unknown. Thoughtfully place the object(s)
upon your midlife emergence altar with intention

around where they land, their relationship to one another, and your relationship to each of them. You might move them every time you pass by or sit at your altar. Simply notice, without judgment, where you are on your midlife journey.

CHAPTER 8

honoring the ebb

Surrender to the way things want to happen next, even though this often involves a vast and terrifying loss of control. Trust the magic that was born into your soul.

MARTHA BECK *FINDING YOUR WAY IN A WILD NEW WORLD*

LONGING

In mid-stumble across the highwire, spotlight on me, I suddenly wanted to climb down, curl into a ball, and hide in the darkness. It is a natural human impulse to crave contraction after expansion. We experience a state of withdrawal after a period of engagement—just like the sea, the moon, and every living thing.

During the years when I was exploring open marriage, I felt I had developed a second heart. Emily and I stayed in steady contact while Craig and I rearranged our principles. While I was closely partnered with Craig, most of my erotic energy was directed toward Emily. I kept Craig informed about my feelings and fantasies. Even though nothing was happening in the flesh, this felt like an important step toward evolving my marriage with Craig. Open relationships can often spark a sexy way for primary partners to bond over such intimate sharing. However, in our case, there was a sore imbalance because I had very little eros flowing in Craig's direction. I felt profoundly heartbroken about this. I often tried to muster it up by planning date nights or fun experiences with him, though, if I were honest with myself, my heart was not fully engaged in most of them.

Emily was the person in my life with whom I felt the most kinship around exploring how our cultural norms kept our expressions of intimacy bound. Walking these edges in a non-sexual way alongside Emily was validating for me, even as—or maybe especially because—she set boundaries to respect her marriage and our friendship.

By nature, Emily was an overtly sensual person, and I experienced moments of envy when she would so easily express herself in this way. Envy is a gift pointing us toward what we truly desire for ourselves. Similar to the internal question that arose as I watched Alyssa Milano in *Who's the Boss* at ten years old, trying to figure out if I wanted to *be* her or *kiss* her, I now wondered if instead of wanting to be *with* Emily, perhaps I simply wanted to *be more like* Emily in the sensual aspects I so admired, qualities I had suppressed in myself long ago.

I had always considered myself a hugger, but the truth is that I had been working to overcome an unnatural, learned distance I had put between myself and non-lovers when it came to being physically intimate. When I was intimate with lovers, there was an agreement that the wall was down, and there was safety enough to explore every possible pleasure. I can fully come alive in that place. With friends or acquaintances, I may have hugged hello and goodbye, much in the way those cursory hugs happened in my family. However, I noticed that when I was sitting with people, I would resist my instinctive urge to grab their hand to hold it while they told a meaningful story or to put my hand on a shoulder or knee to offer comfort. It often felt like I was holding myself back from my true nature. I experienced this as a block where I felt all bound up inside, causing me to wonder if I was emitting a closed-off vibe. While I often received reflection from others that I was emotionally, mentally, spiritually, and physically available and accessible, I regretted that my sensual energy wasn't as visible to non-lovers. The invisibility of this part of me felt painful because inside it was almost always bursting with a deafening thunderboom. In platonic relationships, it came off as silent and tiny, like a firework exploding on a distant horizon. This was an area I was keenly interested to explore in safe friendships and community.

In today's culture, women are taught to be increasingly more arrested, competitive, and critical of each other than we once were. There are whole markets that prey on our insecurities. We put limitations on and boxes around our relationships, as dictated by patriarchy. Non-sexual intimacy between and among women had been sorely missing from my life and my community. I wanted to reclaim this way of being in a sensuous body, on a sensual Earth, with other sensate beings. As Emily once said so beautifully, "To enjoy and to be enjoyed." I wanted to be in a community that reflected the normalcy, the rightness, and the virtue of connection, pleasure, intimacy, and erotic wellness. I longed to be with other women in this way. I wanted to risk prolonged eye contact. I wanted to risk reaching out for the soft hand of another. I wanted to risk deeply connected, enduring hugs. I wanted to risk loving bigger.

Because Emily was also aligned with these ideas, it seemed natural to traverse this terrain with her, yet it was complicated because I had very real feelings for her. Over the year that followed, each casual touch, each emotionally intimate moment, made me fall harder. I was stuck in a loop of longing. Sometimes longing can be sweet. The teacher I mentioned before, Christiane Pelmas, says "longing is the event itself." Sure, sometimes this is the case, as satisfaction can certainly be the death of desire. But unsatisfied longing can also shatter your heart into a million fucking pieces . . . and you end up in fetal position on the couch, binging soul-numbing reality TV shows.

ALCHEMY
Spring 2019

Wanting Emily only felt good until it absolutely didn't. So, I began the intricate surgery of unwinding the tendrils of my heart from the idea of her, untangling any feelings that felt romantic or sexual, while keeping the depth, intimacy, and sacredness of our longstanding friendship intact. So when I say "intricate surgery," I mean it. It was like playing

that infuriating board game from the '80s called Opera-
tion, where the whole contraption would buzz rudely every
time my hand quivered. *Bzzzzt!*

Engaging deeply in my own therapy helped to unravel
all the knots I had tied in my heart, stomach, tongue. I
worked to recognize any projections I had made onto
Emily that may have been unconsciously translated as
desire, especially when coupled with the love that exists
in very deep friendships. My therapist helped me see this
situation with Emily as an opportunity for me to face a
childhood wound. In excavating my need to feel fully met
by another, I encountered a layer of shame—the shame
for having that need at all. That made sense, given the
introject I had received that it was impolite to have and to
express needs.

In one session, my therapist asked me to close my eyes
and notice what happened when she said a particular
phrase, which is called a probe in Hakomi therapy. I settled
into my chair, closed my eyes, and took a deep breath. Once
I exhaled, I nodded to indicate to her that I was ready. She
said, "Notice what happens when you hear the words: "You
have insatiable needs." I first noticed a warm, excited sensation in my abdomen and thought, "That's true, and it's
kind of yummy to be insatiable!" The very next sensation
was a sinking feeling in my gut that said, "I am too much. I
need too much. My needs are inconvenient. It's impolite to
have needs. When I do express a need, people are afraid
they'll disappoint me, so they tiptoe around me." I held
both the delight of insatiable longing and the fear of being
too much for anyone. I learned in childhood that staying
small (in my needs, in my power, in my self-expression)

would keep me in connection to others, in that I would be neither threatening nor a burden. Therefore, I judged myself for needing anything, as if it was always coming from a fearful, desperate state.

This was a timely reminder that our deepest wound often points us toward our superpower, or the precious gift only we can exclusively bring to the world. A big part of the gift I am here to offer has to do with my high bandwidth for authentic connection. I am an accessible, available gatherer and friend. When I give this gift from the energy of my attachment wound, with the fear of abandonment behind it, I experience it as grasping and subsequently shame myself for the grasping. However, when I offer this gift in a clean and radiant way, meaning that I have brought it from the unconscious impulses into conscious intentions, I find that I am met with deep, satisfying connections. This brought me back to the quandary of integrating my lunar nodes: How could I foster true connection while staying in my expansive, evolving, and sometimes evocative nature?

While my vulnerability had proven to be a doorway to connection throughout my midlife emergence thus far, I needed time and space to turn toward myself as a generative, whole resource. I needed time to remember my own eros, independent of any relationship. The second chakra is all about creativity and passion. There was coordination in the timing for me. Taking a break from my art therapy practice at the start of my emergence freed up erotic energy to be directed elsewhere, toward the freeing of my sexuality. I berated myself for not being able to give it to Craig. I saw that to reallocate and redistribute the precious resources of my passion, I would need to call

all my energy back to me for the time being, and I would challenge myself to stay in relationship to Emily and to Craig while doing so. I would not retreat; rather, I would be transparent in my process so I could have agency over my own healing and honor my experience. I would reparent the younger parts of myself that did not previously feel chosen by actively choosing myself now and, in turn, by choosing to love those where the relationships felt reciprocal and nourishing. With that realization, I chose to focus my passions again on my art, my writing, and taking on a vocational opportunity to be a teaching assistant for the same women's workshop that Emily and I had participated in two years prior.

I am relieved to say that I did stay in connection to Craig and to Emily during this time of unraveling. Craig was with me all the way, privy to each nuance. Because of the strength of my deep-rooted bond with Emily and our capacity for honesty, not only did our friendship remain close throughout this time, but it emerged newly resplendent. My feelings for Emily had helped me to uncover a key, golden nugget of my truth. Ultimately, I was immensely grateful for her role as a very compassionate catalyst during this crucial growth point, and we continued to be each other's biggest cheerleaders for our respective midlife emergence journeys.

INCUBATION

I had space to rest and regroup once my heart fully extinguished the romantic torch I had held for Emily. I wasn't sure how things would look when my marriage actually opened. I wasn't sure if I would ever find a lover who was a woman. I wasn't sure of much at all.

Nestled into the cocoon I had created, I waited. I felt uncomfortably pregnant with possibilities for the future. I was laden with worries while also bursting with fantasies about how I would manifest my passions. In that quiet, heavy chrysalis, I was patient for the answers to reveal themselves to me.

This piece of the midlife emergence experience honors the pause that is so necessary in the arduous process of revelation. In this energetic ebb, we turn our eyes and ears inward. We get quiet and curious with ourselves. This period is essential in moving forward with clarity and discernment. In the stillness, the movement we've made thus far can marinate, and what is being birthed can peacefully incubate. Here, we take the opportunity to consciously tend to the ebb instead of skipping over it or hurrying past it with more forward momentum. We can get quiet and be nourished in this pregnant pause, as we are birthing ourselves anew. Often, we find a well of generative energy waiting to burst forth. During this time of self-reflection and incubation, I discovered that the source of my playful, erotic energy did not reside outside myself in any other relationship. It was in the stillness of this time that I was able to reclaim the power I needed to propel me through my midlife transformation.

WRITE

This chapter's self-inquiry practices involve the return to center that is called for after making bold moves. It's time to work with themes of self-honoring, worthiness, and inner listening through multidimensional creative channels. Take this chance to celebrate how far you have come in your own metamorphosis and to reorient to where you are most magnetized. As this time is about recalibrating to exactly what voice needs to be heard from within, the following prompt is an open opportunity to write free-form, from the inner chamber of your heart.

Set a timer for seven minutes. Put your pen to the page and write any words that come, flowing with a stream of consciousness, withholding any judgement or desire to "correct." If your pen stops moving, keep drawing little loops or lines until another word forms, and then another.

Welcome everything that wants to come forth. Trust your inner knowing. Sometimes, we discover what is absolutely true as we press it forth from our hearts, through our hands, and onto the page. Once your timer sounds, read over what you have written and underline or highlight what feels essential to your self-discovery about your midlife process.

171

CREATE

To tune into your personal power and inner guidance, you are invited to create either a wand or a staff. Go out into nature and find a small stick (if you're making a wand) or a large branch (if you are drawn to create a staff) with an energy that resonates with you. Perhaps it's from a particular tree you love, or maybe it has just the right texture or color.

Decorate your wand or staff with anything around the house that will help you to infuse it with your very particular brand of magic. You may tie yarn or ribbons around it; hang bells, beads, shells or charms from it; hot glue crystals to it; paint it; wood burn it; or write words on it. You might tuck secrets into its crevasses or anoint it with special oils. This talisman can be kept on or near your altar, and it can become a symbol for what you are claiming.

ALTAR RITUAL

Stand at your midlife emergence altar and speak your intention out loud for recommitting to who you want to become in this next phase of life. Firmly hold your staff to the ground or your wand to the sky as you reclaim your authenticity. You may wish to both begin and end this ceremony in stillness, spending at least five minutes in silent meditation at your altar, honoring your inward focus.

CHAPTER 9

welcoming
the mystery

This moving away from comfort and security,
this stepping out into what is unknown,
uncharted and shaky—that's called liberation.

PEMA CHÖDRÖN *COMFORTABLE WITH UNCERTAINTY*

COURTSHIP
Summer/Autumn 2019

When summer rolled around, I began my role as teaching assistant in that very same women's workshop. I met *her* on the first day we gathered in June, during an ice-breaking exercise where we wandered around the room while the group leader rhythmically beat a rawhide drum. When the drumming stopped, we were asked to stand across from the person nearest us and hold direct eye contact. In round one, I partnered with a participant named Diana. I looked into her sky-blue, kohl-rimmed eyes. I vividly remember hearing the words echoing in my head: "Oh shit, my life is about to change." With what I hoped was an outwardly imperceptible head shake, I discarded that thought. The leader asked us to share with each other how our friends would describe us. After Diana shared that she was the social glue of her group of friends, the gatherer, the person in whom people confided, all I managed to say back to her was, "I want to know you." She smiled a smile that crinkled up the left side of her face. "I want to know you, too."

As the workshop continued over the next few months, I got to know more about Diana during our councils, where participants shared candidly about their gifts and shadows. I recall only two other heartbeat-brief instances that summer when thoughts (which honestly felt more like surprising premonitions) popped in before I swallowed them back down. Both involved my wondering what it would be like to kiss her. On the last day of the workshop, as we said our goodbyes, I casually said to her, "We should get a drink sometime" to which she replied, "Yes, definitely!" When I sat back down on my cushion across the circle from her, (there are no chairs in these woo-woo realms), my stomach flipped as I suddenly found myself wondering whether I had just asked her out on a date.

In the weeks after the workshop was over, I kept in touch with many of the participants, growing new friendships. As I discovered in that first meeting four months before, Diana and I are similar in our way of keeping in touch with others—we are both the ones who reach out. Given that shared tendency, we were quick to respond to

174   MIDLIFE EMERGENCE

each other's text, voice, and video messages. Our conversations were witty, playful, and thought-provoking. After a few weeks of light correspondence, we did go out for that drink together—I had a piña colada served in a seashell with cinnamon dust that had been lit on fire. In the weeks that followed, our texts became almost constant and more flirtatious, our talks more intimate, our time together increasingly sensual. I was cautious, slow, and deliberate in stepping into this new phase. I hadn't kissed anyone other than Craig in two decades.

It took Diana and me four months steeped in the ceremony of our shared workshop, followed by six weeks of dating, which included nearly nonstop contact, emotional intimacy, and physical affection, to share our first kiss. On a cold December evening, she and I attended a friend's dance performance. She came back to my house afterward. My daughter was asleep, and Craig greeted us cheerfully at the door. They had met one another twice before and were able to have friendly, casual banter. Craig poured each of us a glass of red wine, and we all stood around the kitchen island, sipping our drinks. None of us is the type who can endure much small talk, so when it seemed like it might veer in that direction, Craig kept it real by saying to Diana, "So, uh, it's cool how we're both attracted to Jen." He wanted to name what was happening in the room to normalize it for all of us, though the awkwardness we all felt was palpable. The mutual respect was evident, as well. After about an hour, Craig went upstairs to bed.

Diana and I went up another set of stairs to my art studio, which was in the room over our garage. As we stood in the center of the space, hugging one another, our lips finally met. It was softer and more tender than I had imagined. It felt so natural to me, so very right, so insanely electrifying. As soon as the kiss ended, Diana squeezed me and lifted my feet off the ground, both of us laughing in utter delight. We spent a few more hours making out on the futon in my art studio, under its canopy of magenta silks and twinkling lights. The decor felt just about as collegiate as this new exploration. I wondered whether all of this was twenty-five years too late or right on time.

The morning after my first kiss with Diana, Craig and I were driving to our daughter's basketball game several miles away when I told him all about it. He pulled the car over on the side of the road to give me a huge hug and said a very heartfelt, "Congratulations!" He was genuinely happy that I had the opportunity to physically explore this aspect of my sexuality. Diana and I began dating, giving Craig and me the opportunity to further navigate the turbulent waters of ethical non-monogamy.

LOCKDOWN
March 2020

Almost five months into dating Diana, which was intensifying Craig's and my experiment of open marriage, the global pandemic of COVID-19 rendered the world housebound. Craig had not yet begun to date other women, while my relationship with Diana had deepened significantly. When the shelter-in-place order was given in Colorado, Diana and I decided we would not see each other until we better understood the threat of this new virus. Diana had a roommate who worked on the frontlines, so none of us felt safe enough in those early days to risk exposing my family to any potential threat, especially since I have a compromised immune system.

Diana and I spent a final, long weekend together before we sheltered in place in our respective homes, which were an hour apart. During my drive home, I passed under a thunderous storm cloud that streaked my windshield with rain, matching my guttural sobs and tear-stained cheeks. When I pulled into the garage, I felt like a small, domesticated bird, reluctantly entering a gilded cage where I would be warmly sheltered and nutritiously fed. My wings had been clipped, counter to the energy of the emerging spring season that had me wanting to take off and fly. I sat alone in the "midlife-crisis Honda," parked in the garage for at least half an hour, as another storm surged up from my heart and leaked out of every orifice of my contorted face. When it eventually passed, I could only hear my own perforated exhales. I felt waterlogged and hollow. I carried my bags into the house, one holding the sweatshirt Diana had given to me moments before I left. She had worn it twice over the weekend, so it still smelled like her—a scent of earth, of sweetness, and in some mysterious way, of my own childhood nostalgia. I vowed to put it in a plastic bag as soon as I got upstairs to preserve its scent.

I dropped my bags onto the kitchen floor and washed my hands for at least twenty seconds, because this was the new way of life during COVID-19. The backs of my hands were like fine sandpaper, dry from all the washing, with hints of age spots, like those I remember seeing on Nana's hands. Craig wrapped his arms around me and said, "I know it will be hard for you to be without Diana and for her to be without you."

I was a shell of myself. The ghost of me walked upstairs and stripped off my T-shirt and sweatpants for the second time that day. The first time was when I took them off in her bed so our warm skin could touch everywhere possible for at least a few minutes before we had to say a standing, clothed goodbye at her front door. I dropped my sweats into my hamper and showered. As the hot water poured over my head, camouflaging my tears, I immediately regretted washing her off me. Still wet and wrapped in a fluffy white bath towel, I crumbled to the floor of my walk-in closet, closed the door, and wept into her sweatshirt. (The double meaning of "closet" here is not intended, but it's not lost on me, either.)

I didn't shower again for another three days. I tried to write but lacked focus. I read Andrea Gibson poetry and cried. I ate dark chocolate in bed to make up for the endorphins I was missing by not being in her arms. Every day, I tried to spend a little time outside for some sunshine, as the weather was getting warmer, though sometimes the warmth and brilliance of the sun felt more mocking than soothing.

On the fifth day, the sky was the purest blue, with the puffiest white clouds. The weather that day felt so incongruent with my feelings, with my body. I had felt this level of dissonance before. My body still remembered the glorious weather in New York City on the days just after 9/11, as I had been living there during the attacks and watched the horror develop from my apartment window. The tension I felt in experiencing this beautiful day in March 2020 while the whole world was in fear of the growing pandemic brought forth the memory of a similar disparity in September 2001. I tend to feel bitter when the weather outside does not match the weather in my heart. It certainly didn't match the emotions of Americans during either of these times, as we were all anxious, traumatized, and grieving. I inhaled the ache of it all, then with each exhale, I gifted myself a comforting thought.

Lying naked on my back patio on that sunny day, I remembered how the sky could look even more blue when I saw it through Diana's sunglasses that I had borrowed a couple times to wear on walks with her—walks where I had to remind myself to watch where I was going, because all I wanted to do was stare at her profile. I let my mind drift into thoughts of her. I loved seeing her laugh lines peek out from her own sunglasses. I loved her bouncy ponytail (it seriously turned me on) and her ball cap, especially when she wore it backwards. I loved the curl of her lips from the side and the part just under her nose that somehow reminded me of a teddy bear. I loved how she walked with purpose, usually with her left hand in her pocket. I hardly minded that she was probably pawing sticky wrappers from restaurant mints or loose change. In these early courtship moments, I found all of that endearing, though I wondered if it would be something that would bother me years from now, if I were to ever wash Costco coupons or little salt packets in our mixed laundry.

My attraction to Diana came as a welcomed surprise. Historically, I had been attracted to women who were very similar to me—mostly femme-presenting, mostly edgy, mostly artists. Diana was an entirely different animal. She had the strong, loyal, playful energy of a Labrador

Retriever. She's naturally sporty, having played softball and basketball in high school and then rugby for twenty years. Diana was an avid Cubs fan (while I just learned this year that the Cubs play baseball, while the Bears play football, and I still can't retain the rules to either game). I was a gluten-free vegetarian; she loved eating everything. When Diana saw tall grass, she ran right through it with childlike abandon, while I tiptoed off to the side to avoid a potential tick bite that could give me Lyme disease and alter the trajectory of my entire life. Whereas she liked to spend a Saturday hiking a fourteener (which we Coloradans know as a mountain that is more than 14,000 feet above sea level) or participating in a triathlon, I preferred window-shopping downtown or spending time painting in my studio. When her friends gathered, they drank beer, watched sports, and played strategic card games, while my friends drank red wine, read each other's tarot cards, and made art in our journals. While I neatly stacked the coasters on my coffee table each night before I went to sleep, she could not find the floor of her car through all the sports equipment and random papers. (What was even in there?) I found balance and intrigue in our differences, and I found great satisfaction in our shared attentiveness, senses of humor, passion for writing, connection to spirituality, exploration of intimacy, and prioritizing of creativity.

I realized that I had memorized Diana over those first months of dating, but even more so in the few days we spent together before parting for self-quarantine. I memorized how she had very light, sun-kissed freckles on her narrow shoulders. She had a pale scar on the inside of her left forearm from spilling tea on herself at work a few years back. There were two moles on the left side of her face that lined up vertically, one under her eye and one above her lip. This was also the side of her face that always crinkled up significantly more than the right when I made her smile. Her ears were relatively small, and her earlobes impossibly soft and folded, like petals of some sort of sweet, edible flower. I enjoyed how her small, silver hoop earrings clanked against my teeth and tongue when I kissed her ears, and I wondered how that sounded to her. The soft dimple under her earlobe was a button I could push with my lips to make her whimper. There was another button inside her bottom lip. And another deep inside of her—a smoother part just beyond the ripples and ridges that reminded me of a trusting mollusk without her shell.

Diana and I spent thirty-eight days apart before the restrictions loosened enough that we felt safe to merge our COVID-19 pods. I passed those weeks apart in my golden coop, staring at my phone screen. I oscillated between engaging in delicious flirtations with her and doom-scrolling social media. I switched back and forth between helping my teenager navigate online learning and sobbing in the kitchen with Craig about whether our marriage was beyond repair. He and I would go round and round for hours, only to keep concluding that, as much as we endlessly and intensely adored one another, this was not what either of us wanted our marriage to be.

UNSHAVEN

My parents began their divorce process when I was nine. During that time, I stayed with my grandparents most weekends. My mom had sole custody of me and Kim, who was away at college, so my being at my grandparents' house gave my mom time to herself. One Sunday summer morning, I took a bath in my Nana's bathtub and sobbed into my foamy Mr. Bubble water about my parents' divorce. Nana heard me crying, so she came into the bathroom and asked what was wrong. I whimpered that I was sad that my mom was sad. As soon as I said it, I felt embarrassed and quickly wanted to divert the attention away from my vulnerable share, so I looked down at my very tanned legs with blonde wisps of hair on them and whined, " . . . and I don't like my hairy leeeeeeeegs!" Nana promptly grabbed a disposable BIC razor from her drawer, handed it to me, and said I could shave for the first time.

When Nana left the bathroom, I shaved both my lanky legs, amazingly, with minimal nicks. The thing is, I had only shaved the front side of both legs. By the time I came out of the bathroom, dressed in my red shorts and my favorite T-shirt with little strawberries on it, my mom had arrived to pick me up. Nana told my mom she let me shave my legs. Both my mom and Nana inspected my work, and they naturally broke into laughter because the fronts of my legs were smooth, but the backs were as hairy as ever. As an adult, I completely understand the humor in it, but as a highly sensitive child, I began to cry all over again.

During the springtime of sheltering in place, I picked up the razor to shave my legs and remembered how my nine-year-old self had felt. I remembered how Nana had sweetly wanted to fix my heartache with that cheap razor. When helpless in the face of pain, our first impulse as humans is often to scramble to ameliorate it rather than to sit with someone in their darkness. I'm always learning how to do this better—to stay present with someone in their darkest places without striving to find, or to be, their light. To sit with the heartache and the hairy legs. That day in the shower, I put my razor down. I decided that during the COVID-19 shelter in place, I would not shave, in an effort to experience and accept myself in my natural state—dark sides, hairy sides, all the sides.

DESIRE

Just before quarantine began, Craig and I sat on a small sofa across from our couples' therapist, who specialized in ethical non-monogamy. In that room, my heart ached to admit that all my romantic excitement and sexual desire was being channeled toward Diana. In studying the root of the word *desire*, I found that it comes from the Latin prefix, *de-*, meaning *down*, and *sitare*, meaning *stars*, so to desire something is to pull it down from the stars. It felt that potent, that connected, that destined. I was experiencing full-blown NRE, or New Relationship Energy, a term that has been popularized in polyamory communities to refer to a strong sense of excitement associated with the onset of a new romantic or sexual relationship, coinciding with increased dopamine, oxytocin, and serotonin in the brain. While I was conscious that the NRE I felt with Diana was an early phase of most relationships, I was still helplessly intoxicated by it. The type of sexual energy I had longed for all my life was right there at my fingertips. Turning away from it would have almost felt like violence toward myself.

Whenever I experience something new, it's all I want to do. When my daughter was a baby and learning to pull herself up to stand, she willingly sacrificed sleep to practice this new mark of maturation, staying up half the night to practice pulling up on the railing of her crib. In the beginning of my relationship with Diana, I felt like that. I was losing sleep texting with her into the wee hours when we were apart and having sex marathons the nights we were able to be together. I was powered mostly by the flood of happy hormones in my brain. I was learning a new way of being, a new way to stand.

The intention Craig and I had at the onset of opening our marriage was that we would stay in love and continue to be primary partners and that I would get to have a "side chick," as Craig liked to teasingly call what had been a hypothetical woman at the time of that agreement. That model likely works fine for many people but being a driven, demisexual creature with a wide-open heart, it's in my nature to fall in love—and to fall hard. When Craig noticed the imbalance in my eros, with more and more of it flowing toward Diana, he voiced that perhaps instead of a woman being my "side chick," maybe it was more accurate to say he was becoming a "side guy" for me. We toyed with the idea that maybe he and I would live together as best friends but my romantic and sexual needs would be met by a woman. I watched as he scrambled to readjust his expectations while we perpetually updated agreements. In trying everything we could think of to keep our marriage afloat, we were also letting go of the glue we would need to keep us together.

As much as I deeply loved Craig and fully enjoyed my life with him, I had not been able to conjure a genuine spark of fiery passion for him for several years. Our relationship had begun with our both having intense sexual appetites. My libido eventually took a backseat to parenting our daughter throughout my thirties. Once I hit forty, I was disturbed that I didn't feel strong erotic attraction toward Craig. While I could not imagine a more perfect co-parent, cohabitator, and companion for me, the sexual part of our relationship felt mostly rote. Although we still had pleasurable, loving, connected sex, I didn't find myself desiring sex with him until we were well into the act. We even joked with each other about having "requisite birthday sex" and "requisite Valentine's Day sex," as if these occasions obligated us to drum up some lust. Still, we were having sex a bit more frequently than a few of my married friends of the same age, who reported having sex with their spouses only a few times per year. Some of my friends were completely satisfied with that, and some were not. Either way, the message I received was that this was normal for those of us in long-term marriages with children. But as intimacy junkies, Craig and I both wanted more for ourselves. He wanted me. I wanted the softness of a woman.

With the help of our couples' therapist, we attempted to navigate this new ground. She suggested Craig and I take sex between us off the table entirely for at least a couple months, so there was no expectation on his part and no pressure on me. When Craig saw how relieved I was by this, he told me he felt like I was already gone. I kept insisting I wasn't. I kept hoping I wasn't.

Sex was still off the table when we were in quarantine. On April Fools' Day 2020, my little family of three took a long hike in the foothills behind our house. On that hike, Craig and Diana were texting with one another for the first time to conspire about a silly April Fools' joke. After their prank played out, I saw how Craig regarded Diana more as my romantic partner and put himself in the role of my friend. In our particular case, polyamory turned out to be a pit stop between my familiar lifestyle and the absolutely uncharted territory in which I would soon find myself. That evening, we acknowledged that we were shifting into a form that no longer felt like what we regarded as marriage. The pandemic gifted us with an unexpected suspension of our ordinary lives. During that time, it became clear that it was a disservice to both of us to continue the effort of trying to maintain the romantic pieces of our relationship. Even though it had been happening over the course of a few years, this was the day we both knew we'd be separating.

I had never intended to leave my marriage, and I knew I certainly was not leaving Craig *for* Diana, or for anyone other than myself and my truth. We both saw how Diana was in the role of a gracious, safe, loving liberator of all things I had kept tightly bound inside of me my whole life. Both of us felt gratitude for her. We were moving toward a sort of surrender after having tried everything we had the energy to try. That surrender broke our hearts. Beyond the visceral anguish we both felt when imagining separation, it shattered us to think of sharing the news with our thirteen-year-old daughter.

WORRY

Whenever my sister and I have something difficult going on in our lives, my mom always likes to remind us, "A mother is only as happy as her unhappiest child." I'm not sure where this saying comes from, but to me, it is exactly the *opposite* of comforting. My mom is a first-class worrywart, and I got it honest. (For those who didn't grow up in the South, "I got it honest" means that the trait was passed down in my family, and I have it, too.) While there are a million ways to show love that do not include worry, worry is the expression of love that was overtly modeled to me. So, I get to work with my own worry every single day, especially because I, too, am a mother.

On the Christmas Eve before COVID-19 hit the states, we were sitting by the glittering tree in our holiday pajamas. Our daughter was talking about how she might want to date someone other than her current boyfriend—a girl in her class. Then she asked Craig and me if we ever kissed people besides each other. Craig looked at me and said, "You take this one, babe." Blushing, I answered that, yes, we did kiss other people. The full truth was that I had just begun to kiss another person for the first time a few weeks before, and Craig had not kissed anyone but me for twenty-one years. Miraculously, her response was, "I think that is so cool and so modern of you! And because you two tell each other everything, you'll never cheat on each other!"

In mid-February 2020, just weeks before the pandemic broke out, we were vacationing as a family in Costa Rica. On the last day of the trip, I let our daughter know that I had started dating Diana. She was immediately supportive, hugging me and crying, "I thought so! Mom, I'm so proud of you and so glad you get to express this part of yourself!" I beamed with love and hope for her generation, seeing how beautifully open she was to new paradigms.

As the months of COVID-19 quarantine wore on, I wondered how open she would feel to our new resolution to separate and divorce. Because the idea of divorce brought a sick memory to my own gut, I was beyond worried about when and how to tell her. One Sunday afternoon, I was on a video conference for work when I received a text from Craig. It said, "I need you to come here immediately." The subsequent text said that our daughter just overheard his phone conversation where he was telling his best friend that we were separating. And there it was. That was how our daughter got the news. I was numb and in shock.

The three of us spent the entire evening and most of the next day deep in conversation. While her initial response included a lot of tears and questions, she adjusted to the idea relatively quickly, which I attribute partially to the fact that she doesn't subscribe to the negative connotations that the word *divorce* brings up for me. I have been adamant in not letting her be poisoned by those old associations, not allowing intergenerational and societal wounding to color her lens. Craig and I are writing a new script for how we want this to look, while keeping our daughter at the forefront of our priorities.

In the days that followed, our daughter said she thought she would be more upset, but she actually found herself excited about having two homes. We talked through some of the logistics, agreeing to plan to have a family dinner together at least once a week and to spend major holidays all together, especially over the next couple of years as we got used to the new configuration. Our teenager blew us away with her emotional maturity and her ability to feel and express her sensitivity to us. The shamelessness with which she shared the news with her friends was the opposite of how I handled my parents' divorce as a child, hiding it for years. I am filled with hope when I watch our daughter with her peers. They seem to hold differences with respect, curiosity, and care. My daughter is teaching me that I can take steps toward letting go of my inherited tendency to worry.

SPLIT

My parents separated after seventeen years of marriage and twenty-one years of being together—exactly the same math as my years with Craig, but the exact *opposite* of our situation. My parents never spoke again after their divorce was final, and I've rarely seen my dad since. He and I were estranged for seventeen years between my high-school graduation and my daughter's second birthday, when after decades of my own therapy and time spent developing compassion and earnest forgiveness, I reached out to him. Now, we're only in touch by text or phone on holidays, and my heart is well with the loving yet firm boundary I've maintained in that relationship.

My experience of my parents' split is perhaps an extreme depiction of what is conjured up for many when we hear the word *divorce*—that it is somehow failure, that it tears families apart, that it includes lies and resentment. As Craig and I began to see our way through a loving, conscious divorce process, we viewed our decision not as a failure, but as a success in not abandoning ourselves. We're modeling for our daughter how to listen to our inner voices, how to be in an authentic relationship, how pleasure is our birthright, and how love can change form over time. We are reframing the d-word, as we're continuing to be best friends—in many ways, as close as ever. We've been careful to separate in a way that has been generous and mindful, and that allows each of us to live in full integrity. The shape of our family needed to change, but not the fact that we are a family, still sharing so much love.

Several months into the separation process, Craig and I sat together in his home office for our final video conference with the mediator who had helped us prepare divorce documents. Craig and I held hands under the desk, both visibly tearing up on Zoom. At the end of the call, the mediator got quiet. He shook his head and said, "I just need to tell you that you two are such an amazing couple. I love how cooperative and considerate you are of one another. I look at people like you and think, 'Why are they even getting divorced?'" My heart leapt into my throat. Seconds later, when we ended the call, Craig looked at me without missing a beat and said, "Well, it's because you're gay as fuck." That gave us both a hearty laugh through our tears.

UNKNOWN

When Craig was asked how he and I came to the painful reckoning that we would end our marriage, he loosely referenced Hemingway when he said, "We decided slowly and then suddenly. Like how people go broke." It's true that it happened slowly, almost imperceptibly, over the course of at least five years. It's also true that it happened quite suddenly on a random Wednesday during COVID-19 lockdown when we had to give in to the fact that we had fought as best we could to keep our marriage intact and couldn't do it any longer.

This was the point in my own midlife emergence when I was unmistakably called to trust-fall into the unknown. I had exhausted every option to keep my life in its safe, secure, comfortable form. I simply could not see alternate realities when all my energy was spent holding on so very tightly to the life I was trying to live but had outgrown. As Anaïs Nin wrote, "And the day came when the risk to remain tight in a bud was more painful than the risk it took to blossom." It was a relief to begin opening the unyielding bud I had become. I took a courageous step into the darkness. I let go and, in doing so, I was finally free to welcome the mystery of what would unfold from there.

The midlife passage is unique to each person, though each of us experiences a fulcrum point. It is the place where we must choose to either step back into safety or take the risk of moving forward into an unknowable future. At my own turning point, I often heard the voice of Eric, the astrologer, in my head. I recalled his words about how if we really listen to what we're being called to grow into, the person we were before our Uranus opposition and the person we become after will look completely different. This does not mean we must take a giant leap off a towering cliff; however, if we wish to seize the opportunity that this developmental stage of life offers, this is the moment we are asked to pivot. We are called to make a life change that, by definition, will feel uncomfortable and foreign. It will be a paradigm shift, a step beyond our comfort zones. It may be unconventional, wild, messy, and inconvenient. It will likely seem out of character or even senseless to those around us. They do not need to understand, because it is not their path. We are called to be humble and brave enough to welcome what wants to unfurl from within us, in the service of authenticity, alignment, and a higher form of self-devotion.

WRITE

This unattributed quote keeps finding me when I'm scrolling my social-media feeds: "Your new life is going to cost you your old one." Every time I read it, my stomach flips. I think that's because I know it's true. We must shed who we were in order to become who we will be. In every step we dare to take into the brand-new territory that beckons us, there is an element of letting go. To move toward what is new, we must lift our feet off the solid ground where we once stood. In preparation for taking whatever leap it is you feel you must take, I'm inviting you into some journaling around letting go. Find a quiet spot and grab a piece of paper or your journal. When responding to the prompts below, write the first thoughts and feelings that come.

- Which elements of your life feel like they are the heaviest to carry?

- What/who is holding you back from forward motion?

- What do you need to let go of so that you can welcome what wants to unfold?

- Which identities, roles, masks, comforts, and certainties does your soul need to relinquish to be truly free?

- What energy needs to die to birth the one of you who lives in the highest integrity with your center?

CREATE

Read over what you wrote, and circle words or phrases that you feel in your gut when you read them. Write the words you circled in the first writing prompt onto a separate piece of paper in any way you wish. It can be a list or scattered about the page. You will use this creation for your altar ritual below.

ALTAR RITUAL

Design a letting-go ceremony for what you need to shed so you can embrace this new life. All ceremonies are personal in nature, but I'll give a few suggestions so you can see which fits best for you. Sit at your altar with the page of words that encompass what you are letting go of. There are many ways to symbolically enact this. Here are a few suggestions from which to choose:

- Burn the list of words into a safe metal bowl, an iron cauldron, or an

abalone shell, transforming them
from solid form into smoke.

- Fold the page up and place it under
  a candle, then light the candle
  while stating your intention.

- Rip the paper up, put it into a bowl or jar,
  and smudge the container by burning
  dried mugwort around it. Mugwort is
  a plant burned in ceremony when we
  want to cleanse, release, and let go.

- Purchase flying wish paper or dissolvable
  paper (both available online) for rituals
  like this. Copy the words onto the paper
  and follow the instructions on the
  package for letting it fly or dissolve.

- Write your words onto small strips of
  fabric, tie them to a tree in your yard,
  and let the wind carry them away.

Once you've closed your ceremony time at your
altar, honor the energy you have freed up so that
something new can be birthed. One of my favorite
ways to welcome the new is to sweep my front
doorstep. Sweeping energetically cleanses the entry
portal and prepares the ground for new energy.

PART III

integration

*Confronting the impact
of metamorphosis*

CHAPTER 10

feeling
it all

I disregard the . . . tempo of the ordinary world.
I refuse to live in the ordinary world . . .
To enter ordinary relationships.
I want ecstasy.

ANAÏS NIN *INCEST*

GRINCH
May 2020

In 2018, when we had moved into what was intended to be our forever home, my dream home in Boulder, I told myself I would never move again. After almost a decade of renting places in the Bay Area, my family had finally put down roots. We painted every single wall and ceiling. We re-tiled the kitchen backsplash and installed new counter-tops. We put up some modern, witchy, botanical wallpaper in the breakfast nook, hand-printed by an artist in New

Zealand. We installed gorgeous light fixtures. When we donated our moving boxes after unpacking, I was so psyched to bid adieu to cardboard for the rest of my foreseeable future. Apparently, my foresight was short.

Two years later, I found my life in moving boxes yet again. There I was, wrapping up crystals and candles and wine glasses in paper and placing them into new boxes. I did all of this in the COVID-era vacuum, without much opportunity for the hands-on support I wished I had from my friends and family. Craig was there packing boxes alongside me, though this was the first move in two decades that we were not doing together. Separating from this amazing man was never part of the plan, but it was clearly part of the momentum of the next right step. I found a lovely bachelorette pad just a couple minutes away from the dream home, where Craig would continue to live. We worked out a 50/50 custody schedule, in which our daughter would live half the week at each of our places.

Diana came over to help me pack up my art studio. Throughout our relationship, she had always held my and Craig's marriage in high regard, respecting our boundaries and decisions, and in awe of our bond. Both she and Craig were my constant emotional supports as I transparently worked through every aspect of my feelings around making this major life change. When Diana arrived that afternoon to help me pack, my daughter gave her a handmade card to say how much she adored her and hoped she felt welcome in our family. Then, she surprised us by putting on a playlist she had made for Diana, which comprised the soundtracks to a few musicals they both liked. Diana was so touched that she was in tears.

In the last few weeks that Craig and I lived together, I would wake up to the smell of his coffee brewing, walk into my gorgeous, sun-drenched kitchen—and inevitably, the tears would come. Sometimes, my heart slowly leaked out of my eyes; other times, I violently sobbed on the kitchen floor in my pajamas. Then, I would get whiplash, almost taken aback by the excitement about furnishing and warming a new sanctuary, starting a fresh life where I could become even more myself.

On moving day, the home Craig and I had created together became emptier and emptier as boxes and furniture were hauled into a truck. A pit of self-doubt burrowed into my stomach: "Am I doing the right thing?" and "Did we try hard enough?" and "Damn, this life looked so good on paper." It began to look like the Grinch had swept through that house, seemingly leaving only nails in the walls and crumbs too small for a mouse on the floor. I couldn't believe that I was the fucking Grinch. I wondered, in my guilt and shame, how that was possible. I felt guilt for disturbing the status quo, for rocking the boat, for breaking everyone's hearts. I also felt the deeper layer of shame—that who I was had caused this volcano to erupt in the center of our lives. On moving day, I texted a photo of my empty art studio space to Emily. Almost immediately, she called and left a voicemail on my phone. She said:

Seeing pictures of your empty home is breathtaking.
Life is not meant to be lived quietly, in my opinion,
and I know in yours, too. We're not wanting to just
have visited, to have slept through it. And you are not
sleeping, my friend. You are awake and listening and

*not staying stagnant but moving and growing. It is not
without sacrifice at all. You are doing the right thing,
my love. There's no way for you not to do this, honestly.
Anything can be rearranged again and again, and it
will be. Resurrected, rejoined, reformed. But to stay
in the same place didn't seem possible any longer for
you. I so admire that and respect that. As your friend, I
would not have supported you in staying and putting
it all away and keeping it quiet and locking it up. That
wouldn't have been healthy, Jen, at all. So, here you
are. And it hurts, huh? And it's okay. It really is okay,
and you know that. You're feeling it all. I think that's
the only way to do it right now. It's not supposed to be
fucking pretty, so don't try to make it anything other
than it is, friend. I'm here. I love you so much.*

My therapist also left me a message the day I moved out, normalizing that when we land in a new place, it's like going to summer camp or college. It feels so foreign and wrong, and, of course, we immediately feel like we want to go home. I remember hearing this, sitting on the wooden floor of my empty new townhouse, amidst boxes, reassuring myself that I was home because home is inside myself. Home is also found in those I love, regardless of different roofs over our heads. I had a feeling that I would be apprenticing to these lessons on home for quite a while, and a new semester began on moving day. That night, I had dinner with Craig and our daughter at his place, as we would continue to do as a family each week. There was so much deep love among us, such a feeling of comfort and family that I knew would endure. It's difficult to know you're making the right move toward something unknown when what is familiar still feels good.

At bedtime, my back and feet were sore from moving and unpacking all day. I was dehydrated and heavy-lidded from the exertion and from the river of tears I had cried. I felt a full spectrum of feelings. Heartbroken. Empowered. Enraged. Celebratory. Anxious. Curious. Enamored. Guilty. Quiet. Free. Every color of the rainbow. So much fullness under the June full moon. All I could do was take a magnesium sulfate bath, drink a glass of rosé, and try to fall into a deep sleep under my trusty weighted blanket.

GRIEF

Once the fiery magma of my truth turned into flowing, glowing lava, it was imperative that I do my work to grieve what had been destroyed in its path and put in the emotional labor to shape this new ground. Filing for divorce, finding a new place of my own, splitting belongings, moving out, and learning how to be a single parent half the week, I began a new phase of adulthood. Feelings of self-doubt, regret, guilt, and shame surfaced, and would need to be painstakingly healed.

I was given every reassurance from Craig, even in his own heartbreak, that this was absolutely the next right step in evolving our relationship into new and honest territory. He sent me a text that week that read:

Being with you, being loved by you, and loving you for so long helped make me who I am, and I'm resilient and will grow from this. I'm glad you had the bravery to move toward the truth these past few years. Our path was leading here, and we got to this part as fast as we reasonably could. It's unfolding as it should, and it hurts like a motherfucker. I've realized a few times through all this how important it is for you to hear deep support from me. I kinda forget and get caught in the details and then realize, "Oh shit, Jen doesn't know that I love that we're radically changing things and love that she's finally able to be her beautiful, gay-ass self!" That can only be the right thing to do.

My astrologer Eric often reminds me that as painful as it can be on a personality/egoic level, as one person changes and grows toward the higher end of their astrological chart, it brings those impacted by it into alignment with their own highest spiritual path. It is not our job to protect others from their own soul's evolution. In his view, we all karmically sign up for the curriculum we have been delivered. Sometimes I take comfort in that; other times it feels difficult to apply.

As our divorce lingered in that fussy stage of being legally finalized, when we were ironing out the logistics of signing which car over to whom, and taking names off shared accounts, Craig assured me that we had already done the hardest emotional parts. It had taken us both by surprise that our hearts seemed to be crushed again and again at every step. We cried in the DMV parking lot after retitling the cars, at the notary who watched us sign over bank accounts, and on Zoom with the city courthouse testifying that our paperwork was legit. As our daughter named it, we engaged in a "sad hug" every time we were together. I would sometimes spend an entire day on the couch, opening a box of new tissues, using them to mop up my tears and snot, and recycling that same box a few hours later. Craig would get surprised by waves of emotion and abruptly cancel his work meetings for the rest of the day so he could intermittently cry and nap with our fifteen-year-old cat.

During this stage of grief, my formerly fiery sex drive waned. When I examined this, it wasn't because I had lost interest in Diana or in sex. It was not simply that I was exhausted from the emotional toll the divorce took on me. Beneath the fatigue, I found self-loathing. There was a guilt that my being queer had caused all this pain, not only in my life, but in the lives of those I love. There was shame that I, acting through my most honest impulse, had burned that beautiful life to the ground. Internalized oppression around my sexuality tinged the edges of my thoughts. I went through a period of hating anything that reminded me of my queerness. I went through a period of hating myself. I went through some of the darkest days and nights I've known.

In admitting to myself that my married life, while beautiful, was not as true as it could be, I charged myself to set flames to anything that was not absolutely congruent and to build a more genuine home for my soul. While fires are cleansing, they also bring about a great sense of grief for what has been lost. Grief is the proof that we have loved. Grief is love.

DAD

I had long since forgiven my dad for leaving us when I was nine. That's what we called it in my family: "leaving us."

He had an affair, admitted to it, moved out, and did not sustain a relationship with my mom, Kim, or me. His decision to not only divorce my mom but also cut off all contact with us contributed to the anxious-preoccupied attachment style I had developed since I was a baby, further manifesting it as a fear of abandonment. As this fear came up in romantic relationships in college, I began to work through it in therapy, fostering compassion for the man my dad had become, for the little boy in him who had not been nurtured in his own family of origin. My dad had grown up with an unstable mother, an emotionally volatile father, and a brother with special needs. My mom and dad were high school sweethearts who accidentally got pregnant, so they eloped. Instead of going to college, going to war, or partying at Woodstock in the late sixties, my parents got jobs and raised my sister. They had me eight years later. My dad's parents stopped speaking to him around the time I was four years old because of an argument they had. I've never been told the details, but I can't imagine any argument keeping me from speaking to my own child. Five years after that, my dad seemingly got curious about having sex with women other than my mom, and he broke their marriage vows. His actions were not admirable, but given his turbulent upbringing and lack of emotional resources, he made mistakes for which he did not have the strength to take responsibility.

Once I became a parent, I thought of my dad often. I could not imagine a world where I could ever turn away from my child, which was the pattern before me on my dad's side. When my daughter was two, I reached out to my dad to let him know he had a granddaughter. We met up for lunch at some Olive Garden halfway between our homes, and he cried over the endless breadstick basket about missing our family and about the shame he felt for the way he had handled everything. I offered for him to meet Craig and our daughter a few weeks later. Those two visits are the only times I've seen my dad since my high school graduation.

What was happening in my own divorce would not look like this. I would not be leaving anyone. I would be moving down the street, but my love and attention would stay with my family—with my daughter and with the man who created her with me. They are forever my family.

UNFURLING

In the women's circle I participated in at forty-one, there was a letting-go ceremony in which I offered up the actual foot brace that bound my feet as a baby. This was a marker for the beginning of my liberation. In that circle of women, I spoke my intention to unbind myself and to let go of the bracing I had learned during the time my tiny baby body wanted to learn to crawl and move and explore her world. I voiced my reclamation of my basic rights to feel and to want, to welcome the full spectrum of my emotions, to celebrate my desires, to explore my sexuality, to open to my creativity, and to move my body in any way she wants to move. When I look at my golden nose ring, I remember how the summer I got it marked the opening of my midlife emergence.

At that time, my movement was still sorely impeded by the chronic knee inflammation I had had for two decades, due to that foot brace torquing my legs, making the knee joints vulnerable enough to be impacted by my viral load. Over the few years that followed, as I worked on freeing my inner fire, I became more liberated from the inflammation my body had suffered most of my adult life. Miraculously, my knee pain and swelling ceased suddenly and completely the week after that first piña colada date with Diana. I had been working with a functional medicine doctor for about four years, and after I was freed of pain for a few months, my doctor checked out my biofeedback information using my saliva. Without knowing the details of my personal life, she said, "From your scan, it looks like you're working on breaking emotional ties to past conditioning. Keep doing whatever it is you're doing, because it's healing your body more than any supplements I've been giving you."

When chronic pain lifts, it brings a palpable lightness and joy, even in the midst of deep grief and loss. I was an expansive vessel, learning to hold both. I was learning how to walk without limping. I was learning how not to hold my beautiful burning inside—rather, allowed it to radiate out into the world.

In embracing my desire with less and less shame, I found freedom in embodying my sensual nature and in being accountable for my pleasure. Even in grief, there can still be levity and even bliss. I found myself in a connected, pleasurable, romantic relationship with Diana. We created beautiful reciprocity, solid support, specialized nourishment, rooted friendship, pyrotechnic attraction, soft tenderness, and profound honesty. Among many romantic gestures, I was serenaded with a ukulele in the street on Valentine's Day, challenged with a clever scavenger hunt to find my Easter basket, and surprised with sweet cupcakes on my balcony on my half-birthday.

As soon as I made love with a woman, sex finally made sense. *I made sense.* It felt like coming home. It felt like the ocean. The ocean I had been so afraid to swim in all my life. The waves crashed over me, hard and soft, taking me to places I had never been, but where I wanted to explore, play, dive deep, float. I felt as though I could breathe underwater. Bodies intertwined, with no spaces between. Everything wet. Everything salty. Everything sweet. Everything beautiful. There was something about being intimate with this amazing woman that allowed me to be more accepting of myself, to feel open. I finally felt true freedom from the conditioning that taught me to pander to and perform for the male gaze. Sure, I had spent my entire adult life as a progressive feminist and devoted therapy client working against these patriarchal constructs, but being intimate with Diana allowed what was once a concept to become wholly embodied in me for the first time. Her womanly body held up a mirror to my own womanly body, somehow validating it in all its imperfect beauty, in all its moody desire.

Being with Diana allowed me to feel met in my hunger for a sensual, sacred, romantic relationship with a woman for the first time in my life. She recorded herself singing songs for me, read books to me, whispered sweetly in my ears. We experienced delicious kissing and sublime touching. I felt seen and heard and met by her in a way I never had, but more importantly, I felt met within myself and by myself. I was no longer abandoning myself. I experienced myself as more whole than ever. More healthy. More full. More sensual. More alive. More honest.

WHOLE

This freedom did indeed come at the cost of my old life. With achy muscles and an even achier heart, I woke up alone in my king-sized bed in my rented townhouse for the first time, with my thirteen-year-old daughter just down the short hall. As I made breakfast, she created art for me on a wall in our new kitchen that was painted with chalkboard paint. It was a large rainbow heart with big loopy letters inside, reading: Welcome home. My ache stretched my heart, expanding it to include our new structure. Inwardly acknowledging this feeling of growth and peace, I found myself smiling into my tea mug at breakfast.

My version of the midlife passage has felt both heartbreaking and relieving. I have moments of high elation and moments when I wallow in a pit of sadness. As a word nerd, I love that the etymology of the word *sad* is *sate*, meaning satiated or full. Sadness is absolutely a fullness of heart. It is heartbreaking, as in the heart breaking wide open, to hold more and more.

I've habitually hidden my joy in times that are supposed to be painful. I've felt guilty for feeling freedom or comfort or even ecstasy alongside events where I'm supposed to be mourning. I can locate so many times in my life when I felt I had to hide my joy in the midst of difficulty. In high school, I kept my perfect grade-point average a secret when friends were distraught about their grades. I downplayed my happiness when I got pregnant, because the news came the very same week my sister Kim, who was trying to conceive via IVF, discovered she was not pregnant. I burned with newfound passion for Emily when my Nana passed away, dancing this intriguing dance of grief and lust, with only one of them acceptable to show. During my separation from Craig, I minimized my joy around my new relationship with Diana because it felt inappropriate to talk about it while also deeply mourning the loss of my marriage. While in the darkness of the global pandemic and the sociopolitical unrest of 2020, amid a personal and collective dumpster fire, I felt it would be a disgrace to express any positive feelings.

I felt utterly shattered and completely whole, profoundly liberated and deeply connected. This may sound contradictory, and it likely looks totally strange from an outside perspective. From the inside, it mostly feels like growing pains. In turning myself inside out to expose my most raw, tender, pink parts, in diving into the depths of my grief to fully know its texture, I'm finding freedom.

A beloved teacher I had in graduate school was very conscious of the power of language. He taught us the importance of saying "and" rather than "but" when working with people on personal growth. For example, "I am grieving, *and* I had fun today" rather than " . . . *but* I had fun today." This way of conceptualizing is often referred to in shorthand as "both/and," and is effective in opening us up to limitless possibilities, rejecting binary, black-and-white thinking. We can try saying "and" to normalize and celebrate the idea that several things can be true at once. Once we invite, recognize, and become intimate with all of our feelings, we can experience a new level of personal freedom and self-love.

In my own midlife story, freeing myself from restrictive social norms brought luminous joy, as well as deep grief, self-doubt, and shame. Creating an unconventional, unsanctioned life is a subversive act. During our midlife journeys, one moment we may find ourselves basking in sheer pleasure, and overcome with anguish in the next. In fact, we are likely to be holding these emotions simultaneously. As Walt Whitman wrote, "Do I contradict myself? Very well then I contradict myself, (I am large, I contain multitudes.)" I am in awe of the enormous containers we are. All that we hold.

Merryl Rothaus, a psychotherapist colleague and dear friend of mine, calls the human capacity to hold a myriad of feelings at once "emotional pluralism." It seems that having mixed emotions is a function of any transition when one is moving from one way of being in the world toward another. While one part of us is doing the labor of letting go, another part of us is looking to what is on the horizon. Though it can feel like a tangled mess, feeling all the "feels" is a key part of the midlife emergence. It is important that we do not skip over any of these emotions as they arise, especially the hard feelings, or they will resurface later and louder. The energy that the Uranus opposition calls us into during this time of life is specifically around bringing to the surface anything we have previously stuffed down—desires, expressions, emotions. This is a point where we make an effort to name each feeling and to be with it, gleaning the wisdom it offers in service of our evolution.

WRITE

Grab your journal and answer this question with a list of emotions or feeling words that describe what you are holding in this moment: *How are you . . . really?*

After you've made the list of emotions, let each one be heard. Write the emotion on your page and write two to five sentences that start with "I am" and/or speak from the stance of that emotion. For example, if one of my emotion words is "sad," I might write: I am heavy and hollow at once. It is as if my heart is leaking from my eyes. I want to draw the shades and curl up in my bed.

This prompt is an opportunity to excavate all that is living in the vessel of your Self and to celebrate your capacity to hold it all.

CREATE

Look around your home to find a vessel that represents you. It could be a pot, vase, box, bowl, jar, mug, or anything that truly resonates with your being. You may even wish to create a vessel from polymer clay or any material you like to work with. Next, cut up several small pieces of paper. Write each of the feeling words in the list from the writing prompt above on its own small scrap.

An alternative idea is to use small rocks or shells instead of paper as the canvas for your feeling words. Place each one into the vessel as you write it, as a visual reflection of your capacity.

ALTAR RITUAL

Place your emotion vessel upon your altar. Know that this vessel is now holding all the feelings with you, and sometimes perhaps *for* you in times when you aren't able to touch each one yourself.

CHAPTER 11

facing mirrors

I have already settled it for myself so flattery and criticism go down the same drain and I am quite free.

GEORGIA O'KEEFFE

VALIDATION

My zodiac chart says that the moon was in Leo when I was born. Our moon signs represent our emotions, intuition, and memories, and they govern our relationship to our maternal influences. One of the main challenges of a person with a Leo moon is that we are people-pleasers. We seek external validation. What others think of us matters, particularly maternal figures. This astrology, combined with my "good girl" and "what will the neighbors think?" conditioning creates a perfect storm with vast potential to rain on my fiery parades. That is unless I can step into a more mature, evolved version of myself who knows that she now writes her own permission slips. On a good day, I can rock that vibe, but when I'm at my most vulnerable or when the stakes are high, the child within me panics and strives to gain approval.

As I made major changes in midlife, it wasn't surprising that it shook the ground of those in my close community. My family and friends had their own emotional processes around my metamorphosis. I heard a few friends compare their marriages to mine and Craig's as they watched our story unfold. I often heard feedback to the tune of: "You two are the healthiest couple I know! If you can't make it, who can?" Or I fielded votes for our staying together (when I hadn't asked anyone to vote at all) that sounded something like, "Craig is your best friend! I've taught my children to be sure to marry their best friend. And you did! What more could you want?" The way this landed in me was that people were saying, in so many ways: "Be happy with what you have. Why would you still want more? 'More' is a freakishly unacceptable thing for a woman to claim in this world!"

Yes, I want more. Prizing my personal truth over my habit of needing acceptance was one of the hardest parts of my own emergence. In the concentric circles of my social network, those with whom I interacted daily knew about this transformation as it was taking place; however, I had yet to tell my family of origin anything at all. The terror of breaking the news to them caused my left eyelid to twitch every time I thought of it. Bodies are wise, and symptoms are telling. This twitch plagued me for at least two solid months.

I had been drowning in messages from my own conditioning and early life experiences around sexuality and divorce, leaving me very little room to field and address the conditioning of others. I knew I didn't have the capacity to take care of anyone else's fears, worries, and associations. In particular, the voice of my mom was already so loud in my head around what I should fear, what I was giving up, and all the huge what-ifs of an unknown future. That sort of thinking took me further away from the part of me that desperately needed to grow and evolve past those limits. Hearing the limiting beliefs of others threatened to pull me right back into an inauthentic homeostasis where I might be lured into going back to sleep and accepting that the status quo was good enough. But I was braver than before. I wanted more for myself and for my family than "good enough."

REACTION

Once Craig and I were clear that we would be separating, I wrote an epically long email to my mom. I chose to write to her as a first pass instead of talking on the phone, for both our sakes. When I was a kid and wanted to communicate with my mom about something embarrassing or difficult, I used to slip intricately folded notes under her pillow at night. You know, like the ones we passed in grade school with those little "pull here" tabs. In the little folded notes, I would ask her to write me back instead of talking with me about it face-to-face. This gave me the opportunity to express what I needed to express without being interrupted. (In my family, we are famous for interrupting!)

Just as in childhood, this time I hoped it would give her the space she would need to have her initial reactions and responses outside my earshot. I knew, even from an early age, that I needed to be very protective of my energy.

My mom's initial response to the news of my divorce tracked with her response to most of the big news I had shared with her over the course of my life: worrying and resisting change. When I told her I was moving to New York City at twenty-two, the first thing she grasped for was, "You can't do that! You just got a new car, and you won't be driving in New York! What will you do with your car?!" At twenty-six, when I told her I was quitting my soul-sucking job in internet advertising to follow my dream of going to graduate school to become an art therapist, she said, "But you're so successful! Why don't you just see if your boss will give you a raise that would convince you to stay?" When our daughter was two years old and I told her our little family was moving to California, the literal first thing she blurted out was, "But California is going to fall into the ocean someday!" That last one still makes me giggle.

As a mother myself, I vehemently understand worrying about your child's well-being, and I've learned that worry is not a way of showing love. Even when worry is conveyed with tenderness and love, it does not feel supportive to me. It feels a bit like pity, and perhaps more prominently, it triggers my impulse to take care of the other person in *their* feelings. While going through my midlife transition, I felt like the object of a few of my loved ones' worries. This caused me to share only the lighter parts of my experience so as to comfort the worrier rather than expressing my wholeness. While I cannot control the way anyone responds to me, I long to be welcomed in the full spectrum of my experience and emotions, so I had to be discerning about who could hold my whole truth.

My mom was understandably distressed and afraid when she read my words about our separation and my need to explore my queerness more fully. She responded to my email before we talked on the phone, telling me about her sadness and her love for my family; she assured me that even though our "beliefs" about who to be with are different, she only wanted happiness for me. My mom had known about my sexuality for decades, so this was neither a "coming out" (nor an "inviting in") sort of letter, but this was the first time she (and I) could not ignore that my sexuality would impact my life decisions. She was undeniably worried about my future, about my ending up alone, and about the impact of divorce on her grandchild.

Once we talked on the phone, she expressed that we could "just agree to disagree about same-sex relationships." She meant well when she said that she loved me and would be there for me "no matter what." When I heard those words through my ear buds on the phone that day, I literally collapsed onto the floor of my art studio. I never doubted that my mom loved me endlessly, but I also knew, based on her privilege, social circle, and the conservative news resounding in her echo chamber, that she was blindly ignorant about the damaging impact of using phrases like "agree to disagree" when speaking about identity. Or the way a phrase like "no matter what" implied that I was doing something wrong. It's one thing to disagree about politics, like foreign policy or tax laws, but one cannot disagree about whether a person's basic rights are valid based on race, religion, gender, or sexual orientation. That's not disagreeing; that's rejecting. My mom loves and supports me unconditionally, and I understand that there is also a simultaneous, subtle, perhaps unconscious rejection of who I am.

My mom began going to church regularly when she was almost seventy, just after my stepdad had a major health scare and my Nana died. For the first time in my entire life, she had things to say to me about the Bible. On the phone call after we exchanged the emails about my pending divorce, she told me that the Bible says marriage is only between a man and a woman—not that the Bible actually says that, not that I was even talking about marrying anyone at the time, but debating any person's basic freedoms to get married to the person they love is simply not up for dispute. That's not a difference in politics; it's a difference in virtue. It's entirely personal. It's a matter of the heart. I know my mom's heart to be one of the most beautiful, generous, and loving hearts on this planet. So, her insensitivity in this stance absolutely shatters my own tender, queer heart to pieces.

My inner parent had to step up in that moment and remind my inner child, who sought the love of her mother, that the phrases she used were just protective layers of gunk placed upon her by her God-fearing environment. I was able to have compassion for her fear. I surmised they must be influences from her traditional upbringing in the 1950s, her conservative husband, her circle of friends, and perhaps her new church. They were in the air she breathed and the water she drank. Like all of us, she is a product of her environment and her experiences, and she is on her own path in this lifetime. Her words were coming from the strategy she had adopted to belong in her culture; they were not coming from the sensitive, caring heart that beats inside the core of her, where I know she loves me unconditionally.

That is the heart I see when I look into her teary eyes or see her chin tremble when she is touched by a song lyric or when she's witnessing a reunion at an airport gate. I love the way she loves, and the way she taught me to love. I have empathy for her being faced with something new to her paradigm, scrambling to say the "right" thing, learning to change with the times, and undoubtedly trying her best. We all are.

GOO

Unlike butterflies, we humans don't enter into a dark, solitary chrysalis as a green caterpillar, entirely decompose into goo to reconstruct our identity in secret, and then emerge as a majestic butterfly for the second half of our existence. Nope. Our chrysalises are more like glass houses with the world looking in on our ugly disintegration. We live in communities as interdependent beings, which often requires us to be visible through every awkward phase of our transmutation. (I mean, most of us don't write a book about it like a freaking masochist, but here I am.) Not only can our loved ones watch us flounder gracelessly in rebirthing ourselves, but from inside the cocoon, we can fully see, hear, and feel the responses of others the entire time. Even if the worry, laughter, disdain, or jabs from our audience tempted us to return to our original state, it is far too late. We've already committed to the maturation; we've already unraveled the state of our old selves beyond recognition. We're already too far across that tightrope. We are already mostly goo. The only way through is to emerge on the other side anew.

In my midlife passage, I underwent some of the top stressors that adults can endure—divorce, moving, making my sexuality more visible, shifting my career, and learning how to be a single parent to a newly minted teenager. With all of that on my proverbial plate, I was surprised to find that what kept me up at night most were the projections I felt from those I love.

I realize it's trendy to say you give zero fucks. To be fresh out of fucks. To have no fucks left to give. I can get behind the spirit of this adage in theory—not caring what others think of you, not doing things for appearances and pleasing yourself before others. The problem is, I give all the fucks. I regenerate fucks like a clever octopus regenerates limbs. I give a fuck, and then another fuck grows back in its place. That is to say, *I care deeply*. I am one who feels and cares (and gives fucks) deeply. I am a sensitive being. I faint when I have bloodwork done, and I am nearly in tears every time a dentist touches my gums. I still have tinnitus from my college boyfriend's punk band's shows, my bruises last for weeks, light leaves impressions behind my eyelids for hours, ASMR destroys me, and your words will echo for a lifetime. I cry at the smell of rain, at the sound of fireworks, and at most sitcoms, rom-coms, and even reality freaking TV.

As a child, I always felt like I was a lot, emotionally, and I wasn't sure how or if my heart could ever expand to include all that I cared about. Over the years, I have learned how to carry all that I take in, and how to love all that I love. I never thought someone like me could handle being a therapist, but I also never thought someone could be a decent therapist without giving every last tender fuck. My therapy training at Naropa University was unique in that the program focused on first taking care of the therapist self—how to "hold one's seat" as a therapist, poising attention between my inner experience and that of my client. Learning to distinguish between what was mine and what was not. This was the only way I could have entered the career I did, as a highly sensitive being.

So, naturally, it stung when my mom did not whole-heartedly embrace the sparkly, rainbow, butterfly wings I generated in my chrysalis. It hurt when some of my dearest friends projected their own fears and values around divorce as failure onto my story. I was emotionally bruised for months when a close friend told me I was not being a good mother to my daughter when I began to spend time with Diana. It was hard to hear from others that I shouldn't break up a solid marriage over matters of "just sex" since so many marriages are sexless. It prickled when parents at my daughter's school gave me puppy-dog eyes, assuming I must be miserable without recognizing that I might also feel . . . fucking free! Both/ and, not either/or.

A common sentiment I hear proudly expressed by women in their forties is that they couldn't care less about what others think of them. As I move through life, I'm getting strong enough to be softer, and even softer still. This intention feels far more helpful than trying to toughen up or to give fewer fucks about what others think. I don't ever want to harden into giving zero fucks. I want my soft heart to expand wide enough to hold all the fucks I have to give, to be generous enough to give them, and to be brave enough to follow and express my truth, anyway.

SHOULDS

One of the fucks I gave was that there would be judgment over the fact that my relationship with Diana had overlapped with my marriage to Craig. I had been dating Diana for nearly seven months when Craig and I decided to separate, and there was never an ounce of cheating in my marriage. We were clean and honest at every single step. Though Craig and I had agreed to an open relationship in our last few years together, only a handful of close friends knew about it. Once we separated, I felt like I *should* be doing things differently, like I *should* be single. The shoulds were based upon how I interpreted sentences, glances, and energies of those around me.

When a friend breaks up with someone, other friends are often like, "Yeah, you need to be by yourself for a while. Figure yourself out. Love on yourself." That sounds like an amazing idea in theory. The last time I had gone through a big breakup (which was in my early twenties, but still), I had vowed to be alone until I felt more whole. I had been in a long-term relationship with the giant small-town rockstar, and I lost my identity. In the year that followed, I dated casually, but I was certainly single. I went to therapy. I made art. I moved to New York City and started fresh. I absolutely slayed my career.

This time around, I battled internalized oppression for being queer on top of internalized criticism about dating Diana. I convinced myself that others must be judging me for not taking space after my separation from Craig. I knew full well that it would have been the most unnatural thing for me to end my relationship with her: I was happy, and the relationship provided so much of the missing experience I sought. I would theoretically be taking space from Diana in order to "find myself," but I had never been in a marriage where I had lost myself. In fact, I had been in a process of self-discovery the entire time, and even more deeply during the last few years when I was waking up to parts that were coming alive.

SHEEPISH

When I shared my happiness with my friends, I did so sheepishly and hesitantly, with fear of disapproval that came from a younger place in me. I heard my accounts of joy or pleasure coming out of my mouth in a way that was small and meek. Again, my joy was completely downplayed. In this awkward midlife chrysalis phase, I suppressed smiles and laughter, and swallowed my happy stories around friends or balanced them out with an emphatic "*but* . . ." followed by a darker or more doubtful side of things. I experienced a version of survivor's guilt, going through a divorce and not grieving 24/7. Sure, I grieved. I wallowed. I sobbed. *And* I felt relief, wholeness, and absolute unabashed fucking *joy*!

Ever since I was a kid, I could feel happiness and pleasure, but when the feels got too good, I cut them off.

I interrupted the yumminess with thoughts like: *This is only temporary. The other shoe will soon drop. Don't get used to this. This isn't for you. You don't deserve this.* For a long time, this happened to me on the brink of orgasms, even when self-pleasuring with no one else involved. I would stop just shy of climax and quickly put all the pleasurable feelings away. I don't hear those messages of "you don't deserve this" coming through in my own voice, and they are not who I am. They are products of my conditioning, and, from what I gather, they are quite common in the conditioning of many women. Those self-deprecating, joy-stealing messages live just beneath the surface, ready to be whispered into my ear at the first whiff of satisfaction.

Once I began to share the full spectrum of my emotions with those I trusted most, I realized that the transference goes both ways. Perhaps I was projecting onto others about what they might be projecting onto me. Those sorts of stories are dangerous not to check out. Yes, my friends and family are human beings who brought their own ideas and stories about divorce to the situation, and I was a human being who assumed what they must be thinking. I came to learn that most of them weren't judging me at all. Rather, they were trying their best to support me, listen to me, and help me think through all the gray areas and options. Sometimes, their own socialized values or fears revealed themselves through their raw words. My extra-sensitive-satellite-dish of a being picked up on that and ran it through my own shame around having needs, around being accommodating to others, around feeling like I didn't deserve joy.

FREEDOM

Alok Vaid-Menon (they/them), a non-binary author and performance artist, told a story on Glennon Doyle's "We Can Do Hard Things"[1] podcast that beautifully illustrates the mirrors we face when we challenge the status quo and/or during times of transition. Alok recalls their grandmother responding to their new nose piercing with "How could you do this to me?" Alok goes on to say: "When she said, 'How could you do this to me?' what she's also saying is how could you show me that freedom is possible? Because it's easier to believe that this prison is a home . . . In watching and witnessing you own your own body, I have to confront the ways in which I've outsourced that ownership to other people, to culture, to identity." Sometimes it is threatening to us to witness the freedoms another takes that we feel, for whatever reason, we cannot claim for ourselves.

I was not prepared for the emotional reactivity that would undoubtedly come when I let go of trying to make everyone else comfortable at my own expense. Additionally, I was not prepared for my own emotional reactivity to everyone else's emotional reactivity. This people-pleasing wound was festering and making itself known and seen so it could be brought to the light and integrated, reconciled, forgiven, and accepted.

I honestly felt silly for how big a role this played in my experience of emerging as more myself. It surprised me

---

1   We Can Do Hard Things. Episode 74. Transcript https://momastery.com/blog/we-can-do-hard-things-ep-74/.

how much airtime this piece took up in my therapy sessions during my midlife passage. It seemed like it should be relegated to being a tiny byproduct of the giant transformations I was making. I resisted giving this piece an entire chapter in this book, probably because I should give zero fucks, but projections (real and imagined) from others are clearly a factor in the non-linear midlife journey—one that many of my clients and friends have struggled with, as well. I'm betting you can relate.

I am sure my inner child's need for acceptance and approval will resurface in different ways throughout my life, but the lesson I've learned thus far is this: I aim to grow the space between the moment I'm feeling joy and the moment I cut it off. There's a choice point there. Freedom exists in spaces like those. Freedom to rewire this pattern and let myself stay, let myself claim pleasure, let myself experience unabashed joy. Once I can undo the pattern of internalized shame and guilt, I can start to express joy outwardly without feeling fear of losing connection to others. I hope I can start letting my joy take up space. I do not need to stay small or dull my shine to make others more comfortable. I'm learning that it makes people more uncomfortable when I'm not standing in my full truth and expressing with my full heart.

We have the opportunity to use what others mirror to us as a path toward soul growth. If we seek to abolish the duality of good and bad or light and shadow, we can welcome everything as a teacher and a perfectly timed messenger. It is our judgment of people or events that divides them into binary buckets. Everything in the universe contains both; everything is innately whole.

Engaging in what I'll call "mirror work" can help us own qualities we are not consciously aware of, perhaps due to the adaptive survival strategies we needed to adopt to get this far in our lives. By shining light onto what is not yet illuminated, we can resolve dysfunctional thoughts, behaviors, emotions, and relationships. We can integrate shadow aspects to make our souls more whole.

One way to uncover shadows is to use others as our mirrors. Some people in our lives can play the role of a dark mirror, holding aspects we do not like in ourselves, and some people act as light mirrors, holding parts we do not yet feel worthy of claiming. Both are aspects of our shadow. All they reveal to us is part of our radical reclamation of self.

These exercises may help you alchemize externally dependent irritations, envy, pride, and satisfaction into internally derived self-knowing, self-assuredness, and self-love. The purpose is to help you identify the tender places that get activated by others' reactions to you. Then you can begin to reclaim and heal these parts of yourself, independent of the relationship you have with the person who had the response to you. Then you can begin to have power and agency over the opinion of yourself and the relationship you have with yourself. Remember Georgia O'Keeffe's quote at the start of this chapter? *That*.

WRITE

- Make three columns on your page. (Pro tip from a list maker: You may need to orient it in landscape form to accommodate three columns on a page.) Label the first column "What I've heard from others recently," label the second column "What this reminds me of," and label the third column "How this makes me feel."

- In the first column, list the various responses you've received from others since you've been going through your midlife emergence. Take several minutes thinking about and recording the feedback you've gotten from various people in your life. Resist the urge to judge these responses as positive or negative—simply write down what people have said or done in response to your recent life choices in this transformation.

- Now read out loud each of the responses. One by one, use the second column to write about a memory that comes up in your body, mind, heart as you read each response. You may realize that it reminds you of the voice of your mother or father. You may remember a moment of being praised by your kindergarten teacher. Hearing it again may bring up some of the introjects you journaled about in Chapter 3.

- After considering the response and its corresponding memory, use the third column to write down the underlying feeling or emotion that comes up as you consider the remark and attached memory. This is the piece you have control over and agency to bring into your preferred method of personal growth work so you can own the underlying feeling in order to heal these parts of yourself.

Here's an example from my own journal:

What I've heard from others recently: "We can agree to disagree about same-sex relationships."

What this reminds me of: The ignorance, fear, and homophobia that was pervasive in my upbringing.

How this makes me feel: Rejected, angry about closed-mindedness, shame about who I am, guilt about what I've done to be in integrity, internalized homophobia that was planted at a young age

Now that I've owned my own emotions around this, I can work through them without blame or making others responsible for my feelings.

CREATE

For this activity, you'll need a not-so-precious mirror and a dry erase marker. You may wish to take a photo of yourself in the mirror at various stages of this process to document your work. And you very well may not.

Stand at your mirror and gaze at yourself. Use the dry erase marker to write the words or phrases on the mirror that you have heard from others during your midlife emergence. They needn't be categorized as "positive" or "negative" remarks— just the responses or opinions that have stuck with you. Fill the space as much as you like. Now, read each one out loud. Know that the words, whether they land as flattery or criticism, are more of a reflection of the person who spoke them than of you. Thank the person for their opinion/concern/ love and erase the comment. Remind yourself that this is just that person having their own process. (If the words were spoken by a family member, I like to think of the person using their first name rather than their relationship to me, not using labels like "mom" or "dad." This is to remind myself that they're on their own human journey, independent of the expectations implied by the relationship we have.) After you erase their words, you may now wish to write in its place an affirmation for yourself.

ALTAR RITUAL

Place any parts of the lists that inspire your forward movement on your altar where you can see them. You may wish to light a yellow or golden candle to signify the alchemy that has taken place in your mirror work.

CHAPTER 12

rippling out

Your playing small does not serve the world.
There is nothing enlightened about shrinking
so that other people won't feel insecure around you.
We are all meant to shine, as children do . . .
And as we let our own light shine, we unconsciously
give other people permission to do the same.
As we are liberated from our own fear, our
presence automatically liberates others.

MARIANNE WILLIAMSON *A RETURN TO LOVE*

MOTHERING

Mother's Day came two weeks before I moved into my own place. When I woke up that Sunday morning, I walked downstairs to find boxes that Craig had packed with all our pots and pans and dishes, all lining the kitchen wall. He wanted me to take everything from the kitchen, and he would start fresh. Tears clouded my vision as I tried to pour boiling water over my teabag. I glanced at the breakfast table, where I found a beautiful rainbow card my thirteen-year-old daughter had made for me. Inside, she had written:

Happy Mother's Day! I'm glad Mother's Day fell when it did because it gives me the perfect opportunity to talk about all that's been going on lately. Things will be a little tricky having transitions, but honestly I'm very excited! I mean, clearly it's not what I ideally thought would happen, and I'm sad, but how could I be upset with you? You show you're here for me by being there for yourself. I'm really proud to have you as my mom. You do you, and I can see you're already happier and lighter! I love getting to connect with you, and I know this will bring us closer. I never want you to suffocate who you are to fit into any rules that people sometimes base their whole life around. Honestly, eating popcorn, binge-watching shows, laughing, and hanging out with a lot of witchy ladies at your new house sounds awesome! I feel like we will connect and have a really great time. I am also excited to hang out as a whole family, and I know you will make sure we do. You are so strong and brave. In your being so honest and vulnerable, you are one of my strongest heroes. You're a bad ass, and I love you so much!

Naturally, a fresh burst of tears came when I read that. Tears of relief, pride, and love. Parenting is the heaviest calling of my life. It's my clearest answer to the question "why?" in so much of what I do. I am determined to set the example for my daughter to be guided by her truth, so I need to be a person she sees living their truth. Day-to-day parenting decisions are complex, but a clear intention I always hold as a parent is to rear a child who knows her own mind. Aside from helping to keep her alive, modeling for my daughter how not to abandon herself may be my biggest job. I will undoubtedly disappoint her at times, but as long as it is in service of not disappointing myself, I believe it is for the greater good of our entire family.

When children go through what Rudolph Steiner calls "the nine-year change,"[1] they enter into a period of disillusionment, a feeling of disappointment resulting from the discovery that something is not as good as they believed it to be. There is a waking up (sometimes, a rude awakening) and a fall from grace that occurs at this age. Children become more embodied and grounded in the realities of the world around them, rather than floating in the imaginal realms of early childhood. In making that shift, the child experiences great inner turmoil. This is an age at which a child may lose interest in toys that used to be fun, feeling (and acting) torn between toddler behavior and teenage behavior as they try on both sides. They begin to question the existence of beings like Santa Claus and the tooth fairy and the idea of magic. This is the age at which they begin to see that their parents are not the superheroes they once believed but mere mortals who make mistakes. This is the age I was when my dad left. This is the age my daughter was when I, her mother, had just begun to feel the inner quaking.

---

1   From Thomas Poplawski, "Paradise Lost: The Nine-Year Change,"
    https://www.waldorflibrary.org/articles/1384-paradise-lost
    -the-nine-year-change.

In anthroposophy, Steiner implies that if a child experiences a dramatic nine-year change, their puberty transition is predicted to be a bit lighter. I'm not sure that my daughter will get off that easily in her adolescent years, given the circumstances outside of her control in the macrocosm of her sociopolitical climate and the microcosm of her shifting family. As a parent, my aim is not necessarily to protect my child from pain. My aim is to make sure she is never alone in her discomfort. We ride the roller coaster together. We explore the nuances of her disappointments, as denying or resisting them will cause more suffering later. In our mother/daughter dynamic, we have big emotions, and we have big apologies. Thankfully, she knows by now that I am far from being a superwoman. She also knows that I am someone who would indeed pierce her face—and did. I prefer her to see me in all my humanness—making mistakes, making reparations, all while trying my best to act through love. When those introjects creep in saying that moms should be martyrs, I implore Carl Jung's words as the antidote: "The greatest burden a child must bear is the unlived life of its parents."

The threshold she's crossing as she steps into her teen years is not one of further disillusionment. It is that first passage of awakening and individuating. She is able to see clearly, feel, and empathize with my humanness and Craig's humanness, while being so steadily held, so generously provided for, and so unconditionally met in the full spectrum of ideas and emotions she brings forth.

Glennon Doyle's book *Untamed* was released in the spring of 2020. Naturally, I couldn't help but devour it the day it arrived on my doorstep, as writing this story was already well underway. I deeply related to the entire "Islands" chapter, especially where she writes, "A woman becomes a responsible parent when she stops being an obedient daughter." Doyle also writes, "My children do not need me to save them. My children need to watch me save myself," and "A broken family is a family in which any member must break herself into pieces to fit in. A whole family is one in which each member can bring her full self to the table knowing that she will always be both held and free." That's the type of family we are constructing. It has been a beautifully corrective experience for me to throw all the guidelines out the window and simply define the concept of family for myself, exactly how I feel it.

GRACE

I can count on one hand the number of times my family brought me to church as a child, though my parents considered themselves Christian. Both my grandmothers were Italian Catholics, and both my grandfathers were English Protestant. When I was young, being Christian meant we celebrated Christmas and Easter, and it meant I recited a prayer every night to Jesus that I would have "funny, happy, silly dreams and be a nice girl." No joke. The prayer I had memorized was that I would have silly dreams and that I would be nice. I was not taught about the Bible until we studied it as literature in seventh-grade honors English class. I remember my maternal grandfather telling me that we didn't need to go to church, as I could connect to my god anywhere. For that bit of wisdom, I am ever so grateful.

I grew up in Pungo, a rural part of Virginia Beach. At seven years old, I was captivated by the local legend of a woman named Grace Sherwood, otherwise known as the Witch of Pungo. She was a woman who understood how to use plant medicine, tend animals, and create healing remedies during the late 1600s, a time when this was a threat to the patriarchal political and religious climate. Grace Sherwood was eventually tried for being a witch; her arms and legs were bound, and a thirteen-pound Bible was hung around her neck. She was paddled out by boat into what is still known as Witchduck Point, which led to a body of water I gazed at every time I was in the waiting room at my pediatrician's office as a kid. With the townspeople yelling, "Duck the witch!" she was shamed and thrown overboard. (I'm unsure why it is "duck" instead of "dunk," but that's how the legend goes and how the location is named on the Virginia Beach map.) Tossed into the bay, the options were bleak for Grace: If she sank, she would die. If she floated, she was deemed a witch and would be put in jail. Legend says she untied herself underwater both times they tried to drown her that day. She bobbed up and swam around, laughing at the spectators. Thus, she was jailed for over seven years, until she was released and lived on her Pungo farm until she died at eighty years old.

As a child, I felt deeply moved by Grace Sherwood's story. When I was about nine years old, I dreamed I was a reincarnation of her, and I would concoct potions out of mud and saliva, dancing barefoot in the clover in my yard. The unapologetic nature of owning her power in the face of such non-acceptance was so radical, so wild! I was young enough to remember some pieces of my undomesticated self through relating to Grace Sherwood. When I was in fourth grade, I held a ceremony on New Year's Day, witnessed by a childhood best friend, where I put a silver ring on my wedding finger that would serve to remind me of the magic of Grace Sherwood every time I reached my thumb underneath my first two fingers to hold it. I kept that ring on for so many formative years that my left ring finger seemed to grow around its indentation, later impacting the sizing of my wedding ring.

When I was twelve, I rode my bike to our local New Age shop most weekends. I would sit for hours, devouring books on dreams, astrology, metaphysics, and the chakra system. The mystical women who ran the store generously taught me about the healing properties of each crystal, which honestly felt more like remembering than learning. I saved my allowance to buy crystals and books that reflected me back to myself in a way no one else could at that time.

Deep in the marrow of my bones, I've always felt like a witch—a word that's triggering for many, but that is now being reclaimed. To me, being a witch means I am one who lives in accordance with the cycles of seasons and celestial bodies. I am one who is unapologetically herself. I am one who finds and creates magic in the everyday. I am one who sees the healing potential within herself and in others. I am one who is often situated on the edge of my village, bringing my gifts to my tribe in right timing. It also means that I hold, perhaps in my lineage and most definitely in my body, a very real fear of persecution for living an unconventional life. My fear of being brought to the center of town and burned at the stake has inspired me to *become* the fire. Ever since my dad threw me off his boat when I was six, in a mocking attempt to teach me to swim, I've been afraid of a trial by water like Grace Sherwood. When she was dropped into that pond, she rocked the boat. She made ripples and waves for generations.

WAVES

Throughout my midlife passage, I shared pieces of my unconventional story on social media, the modern-day town square. I wrote candidly about fluid sexuality, queer femme invisibility, holding grief and pleasure, redefining family, overturning domestication, challenging social norms, being the rainbow sheep, and the power of magic. The first few times I posted self-revelatory content, I held my breath. I experienced the visibility hangover of "I shared too much!" until I saw the impact.

Beyond "likes" and comments with supportive sentiments and emojis, I received stories. Hundreds of women responded to me in public comments, and even more in private direct messages, sharing their own stories with me. I heard things like:

"I am at a crossroads—one of the heart, inner landscape, soulful calling sort, related to the death of my marriage. You crossed my mind as a fellow sister who might have some insight."

"I can't believe the resonance in our stories! I am inspired by how openly you share."

"Oh girl, you get it. Separating from my husband and damn the reactivity I have seen! Trusting that things will unfold as they should and knowing that I couldn't continue with things as they were. Working through my guilt. Thank you for inspiring me!"

"I admire you for being true to yourself and exploring an open marriage. In many ways, that's more radical than going straight toward divorce. I wish we had a different concept of love and commitment in our society . . . hopefully it is starting to become less narrow."

"I feel like you can understand me because I'm trying to make a decision about moving my family across the country to begin anew. I am overwhelmed, but reading your posts helps me to trust that I can follow my instincts."

"I know I'm a witch, but I've always been afraid to claim that word. I'm over being afraid to be myself. Thank you for encouraging me to be seen."

After sharing pieces of myself in a way that was real, unpolished, and totally vulnerable, I also heard from many acquaintances, friends, and colleagues from my past. Over a dozen friends in their forties wrote to let me know the details of their separations or divorces and to tell me they were inspired by the way Craig and I navigated ours. I heard from another handful of friends who had been secretly (and a few openly) experimenting with ethical non-monogamy and felt validated in exposing our journey.

Overall, I've had various friends and clients come to me who are making major shifts in their vocation that don't necessarily add up on paper. I've connected with dozens of prodigal daughters, witches, and recovering good girls. In making myself visible in a way I never dared before, I created meaningful connections. I created community. I felt the mutual healing when the ripples of our stories would meet, validate, and touch one another.

I traced common threads in each of the stories I heard from women contacting me. Each woman expressed gratitude for my sharing so openly about things that make us feel alone or ashamed. Hearing those things from one another connects us, and these women were comforted in knowing they were not alone in their journeys. The main theme evident in the messages was that each woman listened to her own deep inner knowing despite the absolute terror of rocking the boat, of rejection, of disconnection, of disappointing loved ones, of social persecution.

MAGIC

I consider the act of exposing my desire for a more self-aligned life to be a form of both sacred magic and feminine activism. Neopagan and ecofeminist author Starhawk defines magic as "the art of shifting consciousness at will." This is the magic I'm up to in my love spells and incantations. When I examine the lens through which my midlife emergence was viewed from the outside, by strangers, my family, my dearest friends, and even the domesticated version of myself, it is clear that most respond to me from the context of patriarchy. I am part of the revolution that is working to shift that consciousness.

Being visible in our wild truths demands that the collective culture change from the conventional to include other ways of being. In midlife, we are called to become pioneers of the mysterious terrains for which there is no map. We are dared to free-fall into the brilliant, starry darkness. There, in the blackness, I have lost and found myself over and over again. I continue to. I've come to enjoy the growth opportunity of getting lost, and slowly, deliberately, and mindfully finding more of myself each time. When we surrender to the darkness, we let go of the patriarchal illusion of fixing and of being in control. We lean in to our intuition and our heart to guide our way. This sort of yielding is our feminine, receptive power in action, regardless of our gender. In Western culture, feminine powers have been bound and degraded for centuries by larger systems of oppression.

Radical truth-telling is radical self-acceptance. Putting your self-love on display emits the energy that who you already are is worthy and valuable, not who you're striving to be after self-help books and therapies and lipstick and diets and Botox. If we all become visible in the love and acceptance we have for ourselves, we can begin to break the stigma and mandate to conform to patriarchal ideals.

I acknowledge that there is privilege in being visible in unconventional truths because some cannot put their lives or jobs in jeopardy by coming forth. Recognizing this piece is key in not causing further shame, invisibility, or loneliness in those who cannot live in full congruence. The more visible you can be in some marginalized aspect of yourself, the more robust the community of normalcy and support will be for intentionally exploited people. I want to see as many freak flags flying as possible. Be your true self so we can all find each other.

Revelation of the fullness of who you are gives others courage to do the same. This is part of the reason the #MeToo movement went viral. When you reveal yourself in the presence of others, whether in person, through art, or even via social media, it empowers others to come forth. Authentic self-expression is contagious; thus, it is potent enough to make dramatic changes in our culture. We need all examples of humanness to be seen if we are to change the media, the message, the status quo. In midlife, we're individuating from social norms and expectations, which I also believe advances and evolves us as a culture. The paradigm is shifting right now, and I deeply believe that standing shamelessly in the truths of who we are is a part of the new world order.

When we trust, follow, and speak our inner knowing, we begin to heal the ancestral witch wound that we will be drowned or burned for non-compliance with social norms or for being empowered around our own healing. As terrifying as it can be, I've been doing my messy healing work out loud in the hope that it inspires others to do the same, hexing the patriarchy by charging it to heal itself.

Fierce truth-telling is one of the riskiest parts of reclaiming our feminine energy, as it threatens to create disappointment or disconnection from loved ones. Some of our relationships simply won't be flexible enough to make room for our authenticity. We could be seen as a threat to people who don't want us to change how they once knew us to be or who feel threatened by our claiming of freedom. This can be terribly heartbreaking.

While I wish I had a foolproof remedy for such heartbreak, I haven't found it yet. In the meantime, I simply practice working with my own expectations around discerning the relationships from which I will and will not receive nourishment. When I know I am going to enter into an interaction with someone who feels threatened by my lifestyle, I remind the little girl inside me that this is *not* a place to expect unconditional love; rather, it's a place to practice using her voice, even if it quivers. I remind her that there are so many other relationships where she receives love. I reparent her by showing her unconditional love. This can be done in very tangible ways, like keeping a photo of myself as a child handy so I can shower it with compassion or taking my inner child on play dates to do something she would love to do.

Superficially, it may seem that in individuating, we are burning the bridge that connects us to our families of origin, but I believe there is an overarching and powerful potential here to heal intergenerational wounds. It is my hope that I am bringing myself and my lineage (both my descendants and my antecedents) closer to wholeness and deeper connection by modeling the living of my truth. I have to trust that if it is true, it is positively impacting those I love. Even if it feels scary to them on this earth plane, perhaps it benefits their souls' growth.

Our decisions, stories, and lessons create resounding waves when they are shared. We all affect each other on more energetic levels than we can see or possibly fathom.

WRITE

Without stopping to think too much about your answers, respond to the following prompts:

- What are you willing to stand for, even in the face of exile, disconnection, or social persecution?

- What gives you the courage to follow your soul's calling toward evolution, even if you must face grief, loss, or sacrifice?

- What can you be courageous enough to say "no" to in order to say "yes" to yourself and what you stand for?

CREATE

Imagine you are the powerful woman who *chose* to dive into a still pond. Draw a circle or image at the center of a blank page with the word "me" inside it. Draw concentric ripples as nested circles inside one another around that image of you. Whom are you impacting in your closest sphere? Label the circle just outside yours with the name of that group. It might be your immediate family or your

248

closest friends. You can write their names inside that circle, if you wish.

Now, whom are you and that first circle impacting with your actions and attitudes? Which spheres do you each influence? Label the next ring as that group.

Continue dreaming into and considering how your way of being in this world ripples out to the whole, until that very last, largest circle on your page can be labeled as "the universe."

ALTAR RITUAL

Find a photo or photos that represent your family lineage to place on your altar as a reminder of the intergenerational and cultural healing you are impacting, forward and backward through time and space. Sit with the image(s) at your altar, acknowledging that varied feelings may arise in you. Breathe through each feeling as you imagine a grounding cord of golden light connecting the base of your spine to the core of the Earth. On each exhale, imagine releasing that which you no longer need down through the cord, giving it to the Earth to hold. On each inhale, drink the Earth's energy up through this cord, using it as a straw, nourishing you as you move through your midlife journey.

CHAPTER 13

courting
the muse

*If you are burning, burn. If you can stand it,
the shame will burn away and leave you
shining, radiant, and righteously shameless.*

ELIZABETH CUNNINGHAM
ELIZABETHCUNNINGHAMWRITES.COM

BROKEN

During the summer of 2020, a couple months after I had moved into my own place, I attended a wedding as Diana's date. It was during the COVID-19 pandemic, when we couldn't gather in large groups, especially indoors, so it was a very small outdoor wedding on a farm. Diana was a bridesmaid for one of her best friends. In hindsight, I can see that it was not an awesome idea to attend a wedding while I was in the process of getting a divorce. But I did, and I learned some things.

I cried at this wedding, and for conflicting reasons—because, like Walt Whitman, I am also a contradiction, and I also contain multitudes. First, I cried because I'm a romantic cheeseball who loves all things sap and mush. When the brides and grooms cry, I cry. When the music plays and when the lovers kiss, I boohoo. At this wedding, I cried for my usual sappy reasons, and I cried for two new reasons.

The one of me who measures herself against social norms and expectations cried. I felt like I had broken everything to pieces. As I listened to the pastor feed the couple their lines about sticking it out in sickness and health, for richer or poorer, I felt like each word kicked me in the gut with an exclamation point. By these social conventions and rules, I had failed. When the pastor suggested that everyone in the congregation would hold these two to their vows, that if ever they faltered or doubted, we, the wedding attendees, would be the ones to remind them—that's when I found myself rewriting the whole ceremony in my head. If a person ever came to me in doubt about their marriage, I would hold them only to themself. *Their* truth. Anything less would be an abandonment of self, and ultimately not in service of the relationship or anyone connected to it. I spent the entire ceremony busily rewriting every line that sweet officiant spoke at their beautiful altar. I gagged on the inside at how jaded I sounded. If this were a rom-com, I would certainly be the classic middle-aged woman going through a divorce. I was a cliché. I was also absolutely right, but only for myself.

The second reason I cried, sitting in that congregation on that sunny afternoon, was that I felt damaged. I watched my girlfriend standing up there beside the bride and groom, in her updo and her dusty sage chiffon bridesmaid's dress, all misty-eyed and smiling. I knew that she had dreamed this sort of wedding for herself her entire life. She had never been married and had never had children. She had wanted a day like this where she could bask in the love of families merging and hearts committing in a way that felt so safe and secure. Sitting there, I truly didn't know if I could or would ever do that again—with her or with anyone else. She looked sweetly at me, sitting alone among her friend's people, and I thought to myself: *I am wasting this beautiful woman's time because I am not a woman who can commit to this institution again.*

If I were to ever get married again, I would devote myself to a more expansive form of love. I wanted all the connection. I wanted all the intimacy. I wanted to feel a sense of security that deep trust and deep love offer, alongside absolutely raw, sometimes inconvenient honesty. Yes, I wanted my girlfriend. And I wanted myself more.

In the context of this institution and this wedding, I was the failure and the asshole, the one who shattered it all and the one who was shattered. All I knew that day of the ceremony, while sitting in that folding chair in the hot sun, was my own clear truth.

I know that I'm whole and that I'm following my own inner compass, which is breaking me wide open in the most deliciously untamed way. If I do get married again, I'll do it differently, writing my own vows and rules, just as I'm writing the vows and rules of divorce differently.

In Colorado divorce law, there is a ninety-day "cooling-off period" after the court has received the divorce filing paperwork. During this time, someone from the court conducts an in-person meeting to make sure we want the divorce. About a week after we submitted that paperwork (on my winter solstice birthday of 2020), Craig sent me a text message:

I have an idea to have a new commitment ceremony together around the spring equinox 2021. Something that recognizes our eternal connection and also acknowledges having space for our relationship to look different than marriage. Something low-key but meaningful. Probably just you and me. Something we work on together to prepare. I think we both want to know that the other person is going to be there in our lives through it all.

After reading Craig's text and riding the subsequent wave of ugly-crying, I envisioned the rebirthing, recommitting, spring equinox ceremony we would co-create. In pre-Christian, earth-based spiritualities, the spring equinox is a time for new life, new light, new beginnings, and new paths and for planting seeds in promising soil. The spring equinox honors the idea that something that has died is now living again in new form.

With COVID-19 restrictions still in effect, Craig and I went through the protocol of having that meeting with the city court in February 2021 via a video conference call. Our mediator said the court conducts these meetings prior to finalizing a divorce to be sure a couple knows what they are doing. I already knew the answer. No, I was not sure what I was doing. There was no precedent for this new form of commitment. This new form of love. I did know we were doing what we needed to do to evolve into our truest selves.

We entered the virtual meeting, and the court representative individually asked each of us a series of questions, the final question being: "Do you believe your marriage to be irreparably broken?" I think we were supposed to just say a simple "yes." So that's what we both said, unsuccessfully holding back our respective tears. I wanted to explain how much we still loved each other and how getting divorced had broken that love *wide open*.

RECOMMITMENT
March 2021

My doorbell rang on the morning of the spring equinox. A bouquet of the most gorgeous, fiery magenta and orange roses were delivered for me, from Craig. He also sent a single lavender rose for our daughter. I wept through my morning cup of tea and then got dressed in jeans and a white T-shirt. I packed up the flowers and a few ritual objects, then drove the five minutes to his house to pick him up. Craig came out to the car wearing his usual uniform: jeans and a black T-shirt. But he also had playfully put an adorable bow tie around his bare neck. He got in the car and showed me that under his shirt he wore the necklace I gave him to honor this time—a silver chain with a Celtic talisman of two hearts intertwined within the shape of an infinity symbol and hourglass, representing the endurance of love throughout lifetimes. I showed Craig (because he is not the type to notice on his own) that I was wearing the necklace he had given me to honor our recommitment: a golden necklace with a sacred flaming-heart pendant. We left our daughter home alone while we drove to the place we had chosen for our recommitment ceremony.

We returned to the spot atop a gorgeous overlook in Boulder where we had held a private ceremony on the summer solstice of 2002, one year before our wedding day. We found a little rock and set up an altar of sorts using the roses, a couple significant stones, a photo of our daughter, and symbols for the four directions. We began our casual ceremony, speaking words to one another we had prepared.

I told Craig that although things would be different going forward, we would always stay close to one another and move even closer, in a new way, over time. I assured him that we have already spent our furthest days apart. I promised that I would always be his family, that he would always have a home in me, and that he would never be alone in this world. I would bear witness to his life, celebrate his successes, and hold his hand through challenges. I expressed my gratitude and appreciation for his being the most incredible human being I know. I would show my appreciation for his being on this Earth and being the father of our child. I talked about the places only we know . . . the nooks and crannies of the homes we had shared. That burn mark that stained the bathroom tile in our Park Slope brownstone because we floated candles in the bathtub during a dinner party; that fuzzy, glaring way the sunlight bounced off the glossy yellow paint in the long, haunted hallway of the first apartment we rented in Richmond's fan district; the weird pink and blue tiled bathrooms in our rented house in Los Altos; that squeaky wooden floorboard by the prep sink in our Boulder dream kitchen in the home he would now live in alone. The vacations we had taken with my 49.9-pound suitcase, the traumas we endured, the private jokes shared with a glance, the intimate moments we had created, the cats we had cared for, the recipes we had worn into the ground, the jobs we had started and ended, the knowing of the characters in each other's extended families and friend circles, the songs that had made us dance and made us cry, the first words spoken by our child, her first steps, her first day of school, her first sleepover.

When it was Craig's turn to speak, we were already in tears. He expressed his gratitude and awe that we had found each other again in this lifetime. He spoke to our magical, spiritual commitment. He told me about how creating our daughter brought meaning to his life, and that he loved how we parented her. He acknowledged that this was a time of transition, in which we were committing to help each other's souls evolve. He promised to be connected and supportive of me through every big event, with unconditional love. He said, "You will always be the biggest love of my life." Craig shared his hopefulness about the future, resting in deep trust that our souls knew what they were doing, and that it was meant to happen this way. Then he read an excerpt from the same book we had used in our wedding ceremony, almost seventeen years ago. It was a different passage from Anne Morrow Lindbergh's *Gift from the Sea*:

*One learns to accept the fact that no permanent
return is possible to an old form of relationship; more*

deeply still, that there is no holding of a relationship to a single form. This is not tragedy but part of the ever-recurrent miracle of life and growth. All living relationships are in process of change, of expansion, and must perpetually be building themselves new forms. But there is no single fixed form to express such a changing relationship. There are perhaps different forms for each successive stage; different shells I might put in a row on my desk to suggest the different stages of marriage—or indeed of any relationship.

We picked up Indian food on the way home for a family dinner. As we drove through Boulder, I felt gratitude and awe at the deep love inherent in the freedom Craig and I granted one another. We created a ritual and spell for release, transformation, and a higher form of love than any I had ever known. I felt a deep desire to grow this relationship from a fiercely aligned place.

While it would perhaps have been more convenient for me to explore my sexuality earlier in life, it's likely that none of these exquisite moments would have occurred. I did not regret or want back one millisecond of the time Craig and I spent together. I felt so blessed that we spent our first halves of life growing together, learning about ourselves, holding and supporting one another. I was so grateful we brought our revolutionary firecracker of a daughter into this world. I wanted Craig to know that I would always love him with every fiber of my fullest Self, I would hold his hand during the darkest days ahead, I would be his biggest champion for all his endeavors, and I would be the first person to open the red wine and put on the hip-hop music to celebrate all his successes. He deserved to have every pleasure and joy of this life, and I would help him to find those. Even if it someday destroys my heart to watch someone else occupy what was once my warm spot in the bed next to him, I have no choice other than to relinquish that place to someone who wants to give him all the attention and sexual desire I couldn't authentically muster, even though I badly wanted to, ardently tried to. I wanted Craig to know that I would always consider him the man in my life.

I also knew during that ceremony that things would undoubtedly be different going forward. We set the intention to have family dinners together, the three of us, at least once a week. Perhaps in the future, others might be in attendance—new partners, new friends—but I also wanted to be sure that the three of us would have special times for just us. I still wanted the two of us to have time for just us, as well. We planned for our family to spend birthdays and Christmases together, knowing someday that could be difficult if we were in other relationships that brought us to different locations or that brought new faces to our holiday dinner tables.

As I looked into the future, I envisioned taking each other to the hospital if we got sick. I saw us attending the funerals of our family members together, someday when we had to face that. I fantasized that Craig would live next door to me, and maybe we would dig a tunnel between our houses so we could pop over when we wanted to hang out. I would help him pick out decor, drag him out of the house for social events, and arrange bouquets for his house from the flowers in the yard.

I hoped that he would hook up the Wi-Fi in my house, bring me delicious leftovers from my favorite tofu meals he made, and steadily hold our cats while I trimmed their claws.

I couldn't see the future, but I knew that my heart wanted to keep the sweetness and intimacy of our family unit absolutely intact. I could envision Craig and I crying together at our daughter's commencements from whatever she chose to affiliate herself with, visiting her wherever she chose to live, celebrating her future relationships together as a family—whether that looked like college or marriage or children, or something else entirely.

Craig and I went to lunch a few days before we got the letter in the mail saying our divorce was final. Every time we hung out in the year between our separation and divorce, one or both of us cried. This time, I was crying about our divorce. He took both my hands in his beautifully familiar hands and said, "Jen, this part isn't a big deal. This is just the paperwork. The legal shit. It means nothing. You and I can be whatever we want to be to each other, as human beings who deeply love each other. We can do whatever the fuck we want from here. That's how we've always rolled, and that's how we're always gonna roll. You and me, always."

And with this, we released the indoctrination of marriage *and* of divorce. We let go of holding so tightly to one another. We freed ourselves from the illusion of control over an inevitably uncertain future. We liberated our hearts into a completely boundless love.

LOVER

I recently found a watercolor doodle I made in my journal when that quaking of my midlife emergence was just beginning. It was an anatomical heart with veins and arteries bursting off the page, with the words "boundless love" written across it. In short, that was the intention I set for my midlife journey. To unbind and unfurl and unfold my heart, my self, in all the ways that felt untrue, and live from that place. The fortunate biproduct of seeking this is that I became my own best lover.

I am a lover. I love. I *am* love. I have come to know myself as the verb and the noun. If I want to be loved in the holy, boundless, sensual type of connection I so achingly crave, I am first to become the lover I desire. At this midlife threshold, where I suddenly find myself dating someone new, I also find myself dating myself. Wooing myself. Courting myself. Pleasing myself.

In becoming my own lover, I've needed to pay the utmost attention to the ways I want and am able to receive love. I've had to inspect my own nourishment barriers enough to know why and when they were built and what exactly these barriers protect. Only then can I begin to let down those walls enough for love to flow both ways. I'm in a relationship with a woman who is committed to consciously working on her own barriers to love. While neither of us (well, none of us) have perfect, unwounded, wide-open channels for love, it matters more than everything that we are aware and that we are trying.

Never mind that popular (yet highly problematic) theory that there are five basic love languages with which we give and receive love.[1] There are as many specific and beautiful love languages as there are lovers. I am a generous lover who attunes to what matters to the ones I love, and I am usually willing to give it. Love is in the details for me, and there are so many ways I want to be loved by myself and by another. Even the act of listing them feels like a love letter to myself:

Write me poetry and prose, mail me handmade cards, leave me dirty love notes in the steam on my shower door, send good morning and goodnight texts when we must be apart—preferably with lots of images (I'm a visual learner) and heaps of clever flirting to satisfy my sapiosexual nature. Please have impeccable grammar. Use the goddamn Oxford comma. Tell me I'm brave and beautiful and hilarious. Notice the colors and textures of my clothing. Ask me the meaning behind each piece of jewelry I am wearing on any given day, because there's always intention in my adornments. Don't be afraid of grand displays of affection and declarations of love—public and private. Boombox serenades at my window, tracing love notes on my skin, skywriting . . . Make me custom playlists full of meaningful lyrics and stirring music. Make me a sexy cocktail when I come to your house. Make me tea in the morning and popcorn in the evening. Make me laugh or come until I cry. Take my breath away, then

---

1   This refers to the book that Christian fundamentalist, Gary Chapman, published in 1995, titled *The Five Love Languages*. The five categories were identified as physical touch, words of affirmation, quality time, gifts, and acts of service.

give me space to deeply inhale the freshness of renewal. Confidently challenge my mind, gently challenge my limitations, persistently challenge me to push beyond what I thought were the bounds of my own pleasure. Read my writing, soak in my art, spend time looking at my photos. Forget small talk: ask me how my heart is doing and listen to my dreams as I groggily recount them in the morning, because dreams are far from boring. Watch my favorite movies and TV shows with me while spooning on the couch under a fuzzy blanket. Take me out for a wild, late night of dancing and debauchery. Draw me hot, candlelit, plant-infused baths when I'm tired or sore or grumpy. Afterwards, moisturize my back. Bring me a care package of soups and honey and tissues and natural remedies and trashy magazines when I'm sick. Plan (well in advance) how we will celebrate my birthday, an anniversary, Valentine's Day. Surprise me on a Tuesday. Give me a thoughtful keepsake of a gift on a random day, a magic-infused talisman that I didn't even know I needed but suddenly can't live without. Sit with me in council, in ceremony, in ritual spaces. Hold me solidly in my grief; hold me expansively in my ecstasy. Get to know my loved ones and love them, too (including my cats). Be damned good at adulting, pay your bills and taxes, keep your home clean, uncluttered, cute, and congruent with who you are. Be on time (by which I mean at least three minutes early). Think big and work your ass off on your passion projects, while holding it all as lightly as child's play. Know yourself as the Sapphic goddess you are. Stand as tall and confident as you're able. Love up the parts of yourself that are still folded and healing. Please smell amazing and take care of the vessel of your body. Go to therapy, go to the dentist, and go to the bodyworker and the energy worker. Relish in delicious cuddling, naked intertwining, deep kissing, melted softening, love making—with the absolute knowing in your tissues and bones that connecting through safe and loving touch is our gateway to the divine—holy fuck. Give me the holy whole of you—I absolutely require both the sacred and the profane. Over candlelight, transmit to me your sacred secrets. Over whiskey, confide in me your most profane confessions. Adore my genuine animal nature; show me your most untethered, undone wildness. Delight in my distinctive quirks; reveal to me your most awkward peculiarities. Be kind, be generous, and be unapologetically yourself. Explore both gritty and pristine new cities with me, but never insist that I go camping or take a cruise. Cross oceans in the name of your love for me. Let your lustful and adoring eyes follow me around the room as I go about my ordinary tasks; let me see your longing. Move me. Show me how you break your very own heart open every time you come up against its growing edge. Show me how you mend it yourself, again and again, filling in the cracks with liquid gold, just like Kintsugi pottery. Let go of what you do not need, of what and who you no longer are, constantly molting out of any skin that is too tight or confining, constantly emerging raw and exposed. Celebrate each of us being brand-new each day. Ask me, "Who are you, now? And now? And now?" over and over, honoring my endless unfolding and unfurling. Know yourself and track your own eternal rebirthing, all the facets as they change and grow in each moment. Love yourself, your god, and the world (they are all one) and you will be able to love me madly, deeply, sincerely. Love yourself. Love yourself. Please, love your fine-ass self.

I write all of this as a vow to be this lover to myself, every single day, even when she does not feel worthy of it. I will remind her that she absolutely is. (You are, too.)

SOFTENING

I was seventeen years old when I read Mary Oliver's poem "Wild Geese" for the very first time.

You do not have to be good.
You do not have to walk on your knees
for a hundred miles through the desert repenting.
You only have to let the soft animal of your body
love what it loves.[2]

I dropped the book onto my lap after I read those opening lines. I exhaled. It felt like the very first true, long, cleansing exhale my body had taken in my entire life. In that moment, I became aware of how frequently I had been holding my breath. I wept on the peach-carpeted floor of my bedroom. I wailed like a baby, and I sobbed like a woman becoming. Everything in me had needed to hear those words, since forever and ever. Every day, I still need reminding of those words, reminding of that sort of exhale.

---

2   From Mary Oliver, *Devotions: Selected Poems of Mary Oliver* (Beacon Press, 2004).

I don't have to be good. I don't have to strive. I can absolutely surrender to the flow, to the mystery, and to ease. I give myself permission to embrace the feminine and the formless. I tell myself almost daily: "Let it be easy." This mantra is often involuntarily followed by one of those long, delicious exhales. A letting go of the belly, a relaxing of the shoulders and jaw, and a deep sense of relief and release.

This softening allows for what is important and honest to bubble up to the surface, making it simpler to do the next right thing or to speak my truth, in each very present moment. This sort of gentle yielding is what I want to embrace now.

This is my hope: I will no longer feel shame for having needs, desires, and wants. I will no longer consider my longing to be anything less than absolutely holy. I will no longer ignore the cravings of the animal of my body. I will be part of the revolution to erase the stigma of neediness. Through this midlife emergence, I have learned that naming my needs is a prerequisite to embodying my full potential. I will trust the pull of my perfectly needy heart, the burn of my tender longing. I will speak my desire out into the air, allow it to exist outside of the quiet, comfort zone of my inner world, even when I fear judgment, disappointment, or rejection. Then I will continue to wish on first stars, birthday candles, and 11:11 on the clock twice a day for that sweet taste of being met. Right. There.

I will no longer question the intuitive stirrings in my gut that have never steered me wrong. I vow to return to my body every time I get carried away, to come back to this divine vessel. I will open to how my body responds in each setting and around each person. Am I contracted? Expansive? Warm? Cold? Comforted? Uneasy? Jittery? Relaxed? All of these are indicators that I am learning to better follow and trust. The body has an innate wisdom I have often overridden with my strong mind, even though my body clued me in long ago to all of what is now unfolding. My somatic awareness may be a clearer portal to my soul than my busy brain has ever been.

Ultimately, I seek wholeness. I want to be wholehearted. I live by Carl Jung's sentiment: "I would rather be whole than good." I want to experience joy, which feels like a fuller word than *happy*. To me, joy encompasses the light and the dark, the pleasure and the pain. I want to spelunk without an offending headlamp into my blackest depths, meet my shadow there, darkness to darkness, and tenderly hold her hand. I want to sit with myself in all of my shame, regret, and self-loathing. I want to pull back the veil so that none of me needs to hide. I want to bare my naked soul. I want to radiate my lightest joy, laugh my loudest laugh, open my throat and sing my elation from the mountaintops. I will no longer minimize my achievements, my self-love, my hard-won freedom. I will no longer keep myself small to keep others comfortable. I will break the lineage cycle of bowing down to those who claim to be experts or authorities on my well-being. I vow to no longer be intimidated by my own power. I am not "too much." Those who regard me as too much may not be enough for me.

I vow to prioritize all that is most sacred to me—all my loves. My own inner divinity. Self-love is holy, god love. My body is church. Art is prayer. Pleasure is prayer. I devote myself, my temple, to the loves of my life. I vow to model self-sovereignty for my daughter. I promise to always show up for her, invite her to show herself vulnerably, share her stories of darkness and light. I will teach her to be account-able, to be kind, to be grateful, to grieve, to rejoice, to love anyone or anything she loves—all out loud. I aim to do my part toward intergenerational healing by not abandoning myself. I vow to hold Craig in the most radiant, warm, com-passionate chamber I can find in my heart, wholly wanting for and with him everything he might want in this lifetime.

I will welcome myself all the way home, over and over. I will bring myself back to the home of my wildness. I am not seeking to be tamed, sheltered, or under the illusion that there is a safe haven to be had. Home is where I can come untethered. Undone. Unfurled. Unfolded. Unleashed. Absolutely free. No pretenses, no role-playing, no posturing, no filtering, no obligatory shit. Home is where I feel I can be the full expression of myself. Where I can throw every rain-bow color of emotion and personality from every glistening facet of the prism that is myself. I am free to be angry, goofy, elated, sexy, crestfallen, introspective, witty, lazy, feral, nur-turing. Home is a place without walls, where I can see the starry sky, where there's a warm fire in the hearth of my belly, burning bright, where the linens are scrumptiously soft and the bath water smells of evergreens and glistens under the light of blood-red candles. Welcoming myself. Welcoming you. Welcoming deep, holy connection.

I am here to risk diving into sacred and edgy depths in relationship—with you and with myself. I will honor this contract with myself above all other contracts, and I will still expand my heart wide enough to wrap itself around

268   MIDLIFE EMERGENCE

my family, my friends, my lovers. I am not interested in independence nearly as much as I am in interdependence. When I am not chosen, I will be with my disappointment and my frustration and those deep, old wounds. I will let the humanness of those feelings move all the way through me, and I will always choose myself.

BECOMING

In the beginning of my midlife emergence, it felt like the entire world was burning, like my heart was aflame, like I was running stark naked through a dry red desert with my hair on fucking fire. It felt like there was no time left to do anything other than plunge my golden staff into the receptive ground of my absolute truth, to unhinge my serpentine jaw, and to howl incoherent incantations and savage spells directly into the prophetic ear of Uranus. I was a burning creature who learned by trial how to rise from the ashes brand new every time she ignited her world.

Tasting hollow grief, smelling seductive freedom, and feeling the gravity of my expanding heart did not extinguish the flames entirely. Every eruption released the pressure I had been under until I could enjoy a slow and sensual burn. This fresh, self-generated heat is the fuel that repeatedly brings me back to myself, to the muse. She is the vision of my future self.

I use her likeness to guide my everyday life and decision-making. She brings me directly into the center of my truth. She invites me to uplevel into my highest potential. She is my north star, my guidepost to living my most authentic life every single day. In my forty-fifth birthday astrology reading with Eric, he told me that I was being invited to further embody this one of me—the edge-walking, subversive, creative sorceress. He challenged me to become her, to dress as her, to merge with her revolutionary energy. He charged me to become more and more visible *as her* in places where it felt the most intimidating to do so, particularly in writing, in teaching, and in my family of origin.

I conjure up the appearance and dwelling space of my future self, checking in with this wise, wild crone as I make vocational, relationship, or even ordinary everyday decisions. Over the years, I've cleaned the items that do not fit this vision out of my closet and home. When I'm debating whether to buy a new article of clothing, I wonder, "Would she wear this?" When purchasing a throw blanket for my couch, I try to envision her wrapped up in it. If I'm feeling ambivalent when choosing what to have for dinner, I ask her what and where she would want to eat. When making a business decision, I check in to see what is most aligned with what I am moving toward in becoming her. My future self has become an internal compass for how I want to feel and who I want to be in the world. In using her image in these ways, I feel I am merging with the highest potential of my future.

This muse is no stranger. I know her well. Her hair is a long tangle of silver and gold, encircled in a crown of smoky quartz crystals. She is draped in rich fabrics—in summer: sheer, flowing, silken robes; in winter: a three-piece, emerald-green, bespoke velvet suit. Neither can contain her bare, soft, illuminated, pulsing heart. Her eyes are a portal into the secrets of the salty, gray-blue sea. She is decorated in celestial golden jewelry. She emanates the essence of a home that is both an opulent sanctuary and a moss-laden wilderness. She is the prodigal daughter, the witch on the edge of the forest, the phoenix rising from ashes. She is the very same inner healer who came to me when I listened to the drumming on that yoga mat in the temple in Boulder at forty-one, extending her elegant finger to pierce my nostril with an endless golden ring. She initiated me into my midlife emergence. She beckons me to become her—to always evolve into more of myself in a never-ending becoming.

VISUALIZATION

The vision of a future self is a guide for everyday life and decision-making. She is the woman you are growing into. May your future self become an internal compass for how you want to feel and who you want to be in the world. In using her image in these practical ways, you can merge with the highest vision for your future. She invites you to grow into more of yourself.

You will find the audio for this exercise at jenberlingo.com/future-self. Use the password EMERGENCE to access this page. Find a time when you can carve out at least twenty to thirty minutes for yourself to relax, tune in, listen to the guided visualization, and tend to the prompts below.

To prepare: Silence your cell phone and any other notification sounds on your devices to minimize interruptions. Find a comfortable place to rest. It could be your bed or couch, a favorite chair, or the floor. Grab anything that makes you feel cozy—perhaps a blanket or other comforting items. You might wish to dim the lights. You may want to diffuse some essential oils or light a fragrant candle. Take this time for yourself to drop fully into the experience. Your future self is already there waiting for you, inviting you to feel more free, congruent, expressed, unburdened, emergent.

WRITE

After completing the visualization, grab your writing materials of choice and free-write using the following prompts:

- Describe where your future self is living. What is the landscape like? Are there trees? Flowers? What kind? (If you don't remember from the visualization, use your creative license to fantasize about that here, in your writing.)

- Describe the dwelling of your future self (include the color palette and vibe inside).

- What does your future self look like? How does she stand? How does she walk? What is she wearing?

- Describe the essence of your future self. What is the other name that she is called—a special name (it could be a symbol or metaphor of her essence)?

- What does your future self remember about the last twenty years?

- What does she say is important for you to know to get from where you are now to where she is? What would be most helpful?

- What else did she tell you?

- What else felt important to you?

Here are a few additional prompts that can be considered as you dream into what you want in the second act of your life:

- Write vows to yourself. What do you wish to reclaim? What promises can you make to yourself as you move into this next phase of life?

- Write your own specific love-language recipe. What do you desire in a lover? Specifically, what qualities do you desire in yourself, as the primary lover of yourself? (My own list from this chapter is comprised of things I've enjoyed receiving from others, as well as a wishlist of what I'd love to receive from a lover or from myself.) Read your love-language recipe back to yourself often. Court yourself.

CREATE

To concretize the presence of your future self, I've concocted a few different invitations to manifest her image visually:

- Draw or paint an image of your future self (it can be an abstract version of her vibe).

- Create a collage of images that capture her essence. You can find images in magazines or print them out from the internet. These may include images of her clothing, her jewelry, her dwelling place, what she might drink or eat, words she spoke to you, lyrics of her theme song, instruments she might play, dances she might dance. They may also include images of archetypes, goddesses, or tarot cards that resonate with her energy.

- I challenge you to become her and inhabit her energy. Go to your closet. Do you already own any items that remind you of something she would wear? Dress as her, head to toe, paying attention to every detail, every accessory, every talisman. Go out into the world embodying her. Take her on a walk, take her out for tea, take her out on a date. Choose somewhere she would love to go. Embody her gait, how she moves, how she stands. If you encounter others on your walk, embody her voice and her essence. If you eat, choose what she would eat. If you go shopping, buy her a little gift.

ALTAR RITUAL

Use the image you created with the future-self visual prompt above—whether it's a drawing, collage, a tarot/oracle card or picture you found, or an accessory or talisman from your closet or home that represents your future self. Place this at the center of your altar as a reminder to aim for your north star, the highest potential you can grow into in your second act of life.

If you wrote vows or your own personal love language, you may also wish to place these words on your midlife emergence altar, to infuse the space with the energy of all you are calling in.

It's all happening.

continuing
to emerge

I want to unfold. I don't want to stay folded anywhere,
because where I am folded, there I am untrue.

RAINER MARIA RILKE *BOOK OF HOURS*

RESET
October 2022

Last Thursday, I was lying on my acupuncturist's table feeling electricity move through my body after she had carefully pricked one needle in the delicate skin inside my left forearm, promising to magnetically pull outdated anxiety and fear from my system. My view of the terra-cotta-colored silk draped across on the ceiling blurred as tears welled up, dripped from the outer corners of my eyes, and pooled in my hair. Before the acupuncturist left me alone to allow the needle to work its magic, she noticed I was crying and asked if I was okay. I managed to whisper through the lump in my throat, "I just want to hit the reset button." She asked, "On your life?" I chuckled and responded, "No, I already did that. I want to hit reset on *the way my body holds my life*."

Over these past several years of moving through my midlife passage, I feel I've been initiated into what astrologer Eric calls my "spiritual adulthood." I am continuing to honor the vows I made to myself. I am following the winding threads of my longings all the way through. I am giving myself full permission to continually realign my life to honor my authenticity. Even with all these external changes, my body is slower to receive the memo that I can let go of the bracing habits and holding patterns I sustained in the first half of life.

What I meant when I told the acupuncturist I wanted to hit reset is that I need my body to catch up to my spirit. Sure, my knee inflammation seems to have cooled. And also the TMJ-D, laryngitis, and all the other ailments associated with having a deficient fifth chakra, the one that encourages our truth to become visible, are slowly healing. I sought out this acupuncture treatment because I felt like my body was stuck running adaptive programs and patterns that she had learned in childhood. New grooves can be carved in safe enough spaces.

The doctor checked my pulse at the beginning of the acupuncture appointment. In Chinese medicine, pulse diagnosis is used to assess the health of major organ systems in the body. That day, she found that the most pronounced imbalance in my system was the load of anxiety I had been carrying. She was right—my anxiety has been heightened for the past five months as I grapple with the only certainty in all areas of my life being uncertainty. I am continually welcoming the mystery of perpetual change.

REVOLUTIONARY

I've also been learning to navigate parenting our feisty teenager, who is a pioneer for justice in this world. In late 2021, our kid began to identify as genderfluid. (This was after I had completed this manuscript, using she/her pronouns when referring to them.) Using new, gender-affirming pronouns ruffled feathers of an administrator at the school they were attending at the time. They were being called into meetings with their school's leadership to defend their correcting a teacher who continuously misgendered[1] them in class. Multiple times, they reinforced their personal boundary by asking the teacher to use their correct pronouns, and they provided resources about inclusion to the school administration. As Craig and I worked together to help guide them through feeling unaccepted, misunderstood, and scrutinized by an authority figure, we tried to encourage them to get their

---

1 Misgendering is the use of the wrong gender signifiers to refer to someone. Misgendering is not limited to pronouns, but much of gendered language: honorifics (like Mr., or Ms.), familial roles (like son, daughter, uncle, aunt, niece, nephew), and other relations (like husband, wife, lady, guy, sir, ma'am). From https://www.health .com/mind-body/lgbtq-health/what-is-misgendering

message across more effectively than via the reactive anger that was understandably rising in their system. This is when our amazing child reminded us that marginalized populations are constantly being tone-policed,[2] needing to soften their language to make it less threatening, more palatable.

Our child then wondered out loud whether Craig's and my encouraging them to temper their presentation was merely a result of our own outdated social conditioning around how to communicate with authority and how to hold oneself in "professional settings." Touché. Their generation is on the forefront of creating social change in the systems that fear (thus oppress) difference. When our teenager stood in front of their school's leadership council to discuss gender non-conformity, their voice quivered and tears of passion dripped down their cheeks. Even though the school ultimately did not budge, inspiring us to seek out a safer learning environment for our child, I've never seen a more beautiful example of speaking one's truth to those in power, so vulnerably and with raw, unfiltered emotion. While this experience made for a tumultuous year for our family, I will carry this lesson, from my powerhouse of a child, within me always.

---

2 Tone policing (also tone trolling, tone argument, and tone fallacy) is a personal attack and anti-debate tactic based on criticizing a person for expressing emotion. Tone policing detracts from the truth or falsity of a statement by attacking the tone in which it was presented rather than the message itself. From https://en.wikipedia.org/wiki/Tone_policing

BURN

Precipitating my trip to the acupuncturist were many sleepless nights ruminating on having the messy middle of my emergence exposed. As I edited this manuscript, I came across a sentence I'd written a couple years back, expressing that freedom is on the other side of the conversations we avoid. I closed my laptop and picked up the phone. It was time to have the difficult talk with my mom about this book being brought into the world and how it breaks an unspoken familial rule around our needing to appear perfect. It's a rule I've noticed that she and my sister have also outgrown in recent years, as life keeps handing each of us new personal challenges to navigate in vulnerable transparency. At the start of our talk, I told my mom that my personal intention behind truth-telling is *always* to deepen connections, never to create rifts. I told her about how her initial response to and her beliefs/politics around my living more fully into my sexuality still stings. She was open and receptive, said I have given her much to think about, and reassured me of her unconditional love and eternal support. It is my hope that this allows our relationship to grow.

In navigating the path to publishing this book, I've experienced an anticipatory visibility hangover about sharing my story with a wider audience. It is as though I am willfully putting myself up on the stake in the town square, risking public execution (even if the modern version of that is an unfavorable Amazon review) for voicing the more subversive aspects of my life. I'm trusting that I cannot be burned at the stake if I become the fire itself, but the fear of persecution lives in the nucleus of each cell of my body, perhaps from past lifetimes, from epigenetics, or from familiar situations in this lifetime. I am soothed only when I can remember that my work in this world is to make the unconscious conscious, to tell the truth, and to evolve past old ways of being that no longer serve the personal, thus the collective.

LUSH

Last week, after that single acupuncture needle had been dutifully employed in my arm for about twenty minutes, I noticed I had been involuntarily smiling at the amber light fixture hanging above me. I physically felt a noticeable release and an unraveling. As I lay there alone in the warmth of the treatment room, simultaneously smiling and crying, I wondered where else in my life I get to experience the relief of such unwinding. The answer came immediately. I recognize myself as me, as whole unto myself, when I am making love with Diana. It's when old layers of anxiety, fear, posturing, and protection are peeled back. I get to unfurl into the unbound, unbraced wildness of who I have incarnated to be. It feels sacred and holy. I am endlessly grateful that she and I can create a safe enough container for me to fully see and meet myself in this way. And, as I cannot be entangled with her in every moment of my life, I am dedicated to expanding this container more widely. I aim to be secure enough inside myself that I can unfold in my true form in any environment and in any company that feels worthy of my truth. I use the feelings that arise on the acupuncture table and with Diana as a touchpoint, so that I may continue to reveal this core of myself. That is what I am up to these days: placing my attention on what is *aligned*, what is *honest*, what is *love*. I amplify these verdant parts as I continue to integrate and merge with the essence of my future self.

Astrologers and developmental psychologists say we are called into the zenith of our midlife transition around age forty-two, which is indeed when my own quivering mountain of midlife fully erupted. Through this, I have learned firsthand that beyond being destructive, fire is also cleansing and enlightening. Today, as I near my forty-seventh birthday on the winter solstice, my own fire seems to take the form of the smooth, viscous flow of fully expressed, ropy lava. Still warm and lit from within, it forms new, solid ground as it takes up more space. Some of the lushest places on earth are growing upon volcanic land.

acknowledgments

Thank you to my team at Bold Story Press for helping me bring my story to the world. To Emily Barrosse for your guidance and vision, to Julianna Scott Fein for being such a thorough and dependable J, to Nedah Rose for making this a better book, to Karen Polaski for understanding my passion for the visuals.

To Jewel Afflerbaugh for seeing my fire through your lens.

To Nirmala Nataraj for your valuable feedback on my first draft in helping me to organize all these big feelings into stories. To Courtney, Jen, and Sara for your early and honest input.

To the gifted healing practitioners in my life: Dr. Jen, Dr. Miller, Dr. Hulse, Anne-Marie, Stephanie, Deirdre, and Eve. And to Eric Meyers for gently yet firmly holding me to the high end of my chart and for being an advocate for bringing forth the parts of me that are mad-Scorpionic.

To the CYM circles of 2017 and 2019 for helping reflect my medicine back to me and watching me painfully labor through its birth.

To my family of origin (and my ancestors before them) for being the perfect family for me to be born into. You are helping me to become.

To Emily for exploring the edges of radical territory alongside me. And along with the rest of my coven,

Gretchen, Molly, and Rachel, for holding me in my most tender and powerful moments. (They're often the same.)

To Diana for witnessing me as I meet that place within myself that has deeply longed to be met ever since I was that lonely little girl in the nook of my favorite tree. For the way you love, in full integrity.

To Craig for ardently, patiently, generously teaching me that big love feels like freedom, for always reminding me about the core of who I am under any bullshit layers, and for being the most loving dad in the universe to the lightning bolt of a person we created.

To my revolutionary, pioneering, courageous child for being a force of radiant love in this world and in my life. You've taught me how to question my own conditioning more than any other human.

I love you all endlessly,
jen

about the author

Jen Berlingo, MA, LPC, ATR (she/her) is a midlife coach, a licensed professional counselor in the state of Colorado, a nationally registered art therapist, and a master-level Reiki practitioner. She earned her graduate's degree in transpersonal counseling psychology and art therapy from Naropa University, a Buddhist-oriented school for experiential and contemplative education. For twenty years, she has used coaching, counseling, art psychotherapy, energy work, ritual, and ceremony to support women in becoming their most authentic, sovereign selves. Through her private practice, women's circles, and online programs, Jen has midwifed hundreds of women through life's turning points, as they rebirth and re-parent themselves into more fully expressed, whole beings.

While guiding clients through cathartic metamorphoses and quests for true alignment, Jen experienced her own profoundly transformative passage in her forties, where she was able to expand more fully into her queer identity and embrace other seemingly subversive aspects of herself. Jen's journey inspired her to write *Midlife Emergence* to accompany other women in traversing the midlife portal. She invites the often inconvenient, raw truth to come forward in service of alchemizing shame into powerful reclamation.

In addition to her longstanding work as a healing practitioner, Jen is a visual artist who offers original paintings, prints, and oracle decks to collectors worldwide. She exhibits her fluid, abstract art locally in her beloved town of Boulder, Colorado. There, among the sunny foothills, Jen can be found making bottomless bowls of popcorn and snuggling on the couch with her unconventional family, her coven of close friends, and her Norwegian forest tabby rescues, Jinx and Juju. Learn more about Jen and her offerings by visiting jenberlingo.com.

about bold story press

Bold Story Press is a curated, woman-owned hybrid publishing company with a mission of publishing well-written
stories by women. If your book is chosen for publication,
our team of expert editors and designers will work with
you to publish a professionally edited and designed book.
Every woman has a story to tell. If you have written yours
and want to explore publishing with Bold Story Press, contact us at https://boldstorypress.com.

**BOLD
STORY
PRESS**

The Bold Story Press logo, designed by Grace Arsenault,
was inspired by the nom de plume, or pen name, a sad
necessity at one time for female authors who wanted to
publish. The woman's face hidden in the quill is the profile
of Virginia Woolf, who, in addition to being an early feminist writer, founded and ran her own publishing company,
Hogarth Press.

Made in United States
Orlando, FL
13 June 2023

34070579R00183